NEW JERSEY
in the
JAZZ AGE

JOSEPH BILBY & HARRY ZIEGLER

THE
History
PRESS

Published by The History Press
Charleston, SC
www.historypress.com

First published 2025

Manufactured in the United States

ISBN 9781467158664

Library of Congress Control Number: 2024947367

So we beat on, boats against the current, borne back ceaselessly into the past.
—*F. Scott Fitzgerald,* The Great Gatsby

If time were suddenly to turn back to the earliest days of the Post War Decade, and you were to look about you, what would seem strange to you? Since 1919 the circumstances of American life have been transformed—yes, but exactly how?
—*Frederick Lewis Allen,*
Only Yesterday: An Informal History of the 1920s

We wish to dedicate this book to the members of our families, longtime New Jerseyans, who are no longer with us but who experienced the state's long-ago Jazz Age in person.

CONTENTS

INTRODUCTION

I t all started with the end of a global conflict that, for better or worse (mostly the latter), provided the first step into the modern era.[1] The world was dramatically different than it had been prior to World War I, the catastrophic conflict blundered into by European monarchs who should have known better. By 1920, the war was over for the Europeans—or at least they thought so—but it was theoretically still on for America, until it ended in a New Jersey living room where President Harding signed a paper after a golf game. The American concept of the "Great War" had transitioned from a super patriotic propaganda exercise, managed by president and former New Jersey governor Woodrow Wilson and his toady James Creel, to what many Americans considered a bloody struggle to maintain and expand colonial empires, in which Americans were used as tools by European leaders.

The war laid the groundwork for significant cultural change in America, however. Prohibitionists finally got a foothold in the political hierarchy with the official denial of alcoholic beverage sales to or use by soldiers, which led to volunteer spies hanging out in Hoboken bars and strolling around the National Guard camp at Sea Girt, hoping to catch soldiers imbibing. Woodrow Wilson, a former opponent of women's suffrage who had New Jersey suffragist Alice Paul and others jailed, released them and endorsed the movement in the hopes of gaining their support for American participation in the conflict.

And then, when actual combat ended, it all came crashing down for the United States. The Senate would not approve the Treaty of Versailles; New

World War I propaganda poster aimed at New Jerseyans.

Jersey governor Edward Edwards promised to keep the state as wet as the Atlantic Ocean, to no avail; President Wilson suffered a severe stroke; and the country was essentially run by his wife, Edith, and advisor, Jersey City attorney Joseph Patrick Tumulty, who hated each other. Nucky Johnson and Frank Hague ran New Jersey politics, the Ku Klux Klan came back to life, automobiles and planes became growing sources of transportation to the average American, murder trials became spectator sports and William "Count" Basie began to hang out at the Palace Theatre in Red Bank. It would be an interesting decade.

We make no claim to covering every story of 1920s New Jersey, but we have selected a number of them that reflect the cultural transitions of the era. Enjoy!

Chapter 1

POLITICS

In 1919, Edward I. Edwards of Jersey City was running for New Jersey governor as a Democrat. Should he win the nomination and election, Edwards, a banker and attorney who had served as the state's comptroller of the treasury during the Woodrow Wilson governorship and subsequently as a New Jersey state senator, would assume office in January 1920, the thirty-seventh governor of the state and first governor of a new decade. Whether or not he was aware of the forthcoming changes to the state and nation in that decade, aside from the imminent establishment of Prohibition, which he made a campaign issue, is unknown.[2]

It was indeed the eve of a tumultuous era. There were changes impending in the social and political order. The *Penn's Grove Record* condemned Edward's primary opponent, attorney and legislator James R. Nugent of Newark, for belonging in New Jersey's "past generation of boodle booze bosses." According to the paper, Nugent was a "notorious lobbyist at Trenton for brewers and saloon keepers," who, when he was corporation counsel for Newark, had "used all of his power to protect disorderly houses [brothels] whose proprietors were sent to the penitentiary and publicly recommended that the persons who had exposed those criminals be 'driven out of town.'" The editorial concluded with the recommendation that "Edwards is the man to vote for for [*sic*] Governor in the Democratic primary."[3]

Edwards was an associate of Jersey City mayor Frank Hague, who was elected to his first term by the City Council in 1917. Although Hague was, at the time, relatively unknown outside Hudson County, he would become the most famous and powerful political boss in New Jersey history in the years to come. His Republican counterpart, Enoch "Nucky" Johnson of Atlantic City, who was portrayed in an exaggerated form in the excellent HBO series *Boardwalk Empire*, had already assisted Walter Evans Edge into the statehouse. Both bosses would occasionally cooperate in the future.

Edwards went on to win the nomination, and in an October 18, 1919 speech at Perth Amboy while running for governor, he promised the people of New Jersey that, despite the ratification of the Eighteenth Amendment on January 16, 1919, with Prohibition of alcohol sales due to begin at midnight, January 17, 1920, he would keep the state "as wet as the Atlantic Ocean."[4]

Edwards won the election over Republican state comptroller Newton Bugbee and was inaugurated on January 20, 1920. After some allusions to "states' rights," which his opponent had advised him was an issue settled in 1865, Edwards tried several lackluster efforts to keep New Jersey legally "wet," including an attempt to make beer with a 2.5 alcohol level legal, but failed in court. Edwards, ironically, abstained from liquor himself. Despite the governor's unfulfilled promise, New Jersey, as you shall see in our chapter on Prohibition, was more than damp for the next decade.[5] One of Edwards's chief achievements was to sponsor and sign a state bonus for World War I veterans.

There were problems with Jersey rungs up the political ladder as well, which affected the performance of the Edwards governorship and the rest of the decade. President Woodrow Wilson, a former New Jersey governor, had a reputation as a progressive, but his policies varied. He was born in the South and spent his early years in the Confederacy, and some say his father was a chaplain in the Confederate army. His progressive side was reflected in policies like a reduction in tariffs to make imported goods more affordable to average Americans, natural resources conservation and bank reforms and an income tax, but on his arrival in Washington in 1913, he racially segregated government workers. Wilson was also against women's suffrage and had women activists, among them Jersey Girl Alice Paul, arrested and jailed for demonstrating at the White House.[6]

World War I had erupted in Europe in 1914, and Wilson declared the United States as neutral, although the country, in particular New Jersey, supplied ammunition to the Allies. The state suffered several massive sabotage incidents, including Black Tom ammunition pier on Jersey City in 1916 and the Kingsland ammunition plant in Lyndhurst in 1917, as well as a number of other explosions caused by manufacturing errors. By 1917, New Jersey was the largest ammunition-producing state in the country.

Left: New Jersey governor Edward Edwards (*left*) and Jersey City political boss Frank Hague at a post-election party in 1920.

Right: Alice Paul, New Jersey's leading suffragist.

There was a downside to a profitable but inherently dangerous industry, however. Although not all due to saboteurs, the explosions continued for years afterward. One of the most notable was at Lake Denmark, six years into the new decade. The United States War Department established Picatinny Powder Depot, near Dover, New Jersey, in September 1880. Located in a valley and bordering Lake Denmark and Lake Picatinny, it was intended to be a centralized gunpowder storage center. In 1891, the army transferred 315 acres on Lake Denmark to the navy.

In 1907, the depot's name was changed to Picatinny Arsenal. A gunpowder manufacturing facility was erected on the site, and the arsenal also began ammunition research and development work. An ordnance school for officers was established at Picatinny in 1911. During World War I, the arsenal created a testing program for ammunition and began to design and experiment with artillery shells and fuses.

On July 10, 1926, lightning struck a navy ammunition warehouse at Lake Denmark. The resulting fire exploded several million pounds of explosives in a chain reaction lasting several days, resulting in massive

Opposite, top: Alice Paul's suffragists picketing in front of the White House after President Wilson agreed to support their ability to vote in exchange for their support for his declaration of war on Germany in 1917.

Opposite, bottom: The 1916 sabotage explosion of Black Tom Island, the Jersey City dock transporting ammunition to Europe.

Above: Burning buildings at the Kingsland Ammunition plant in Lyndhurst, sabotaged in 1917.

structural damage—187 out of 200 buildings were destroyed—and many casualties. After recovering from the devastation, Picatinny's personnel continued work on processing and storing smokeless power, as well as conducting tests.

Woodrow Wilson ran for a second presidential term in 1916, with his campaign headquarters in Asbury Park and campaign residence at Shadow Lawn mansion in West Long Branch, New Jersey, using the slogan "He kept us out of War." He won reelection. Shortly after his March 1917 inauguration, however, Wilson asked Congress to declare war on Germany, basing his instruction on the fact that Germany had resumed unrestricted submarine warfare in January. Wilson also met with Alice Paul and endorsed women's suffrage to gain the support of suffragists for intervention in the European war.[7]

In January 1918, Wilson published his Fourteen Points, a guideline to a lasting peace—or so he thought. He subsequently traveled to Europe to engage, along with other Allied leaders, in peace talks. This resulted in the Versailles Treaty, which included Wilson's idea of the League of Nations, with national representatives from around the world. The British and French leaders preferred to increase their colonial empires and punish Germany and more or less humored the American president's view of the world, although the League was created as an integral part of the treaty.

When he returned to the United States, Wilson, who had disdained congressional engagement on the treaty talks and squabbled with Democrats in Congress regarding interpretations of parts of the treaty, found, to his dismay, that the election of 1918 had returned Republicans to control of Congress. Congress rejected both the treaty and membership in the League. A recent book laid much of the blame on Wilson's mental illness, referring to his failure to even attempt to compromise with Congress and his confidence that he was doing God's Work. Economist John Maynard Keynes referred to Wilson as "a blind and deaf Don Quixote."[8]

In October 1919, Wilson suffered a stroke and was cared for by his second wife, Edith. His first wife, Ellen, had died in 1914, and Wilson, recently widowed, was being chauffeured down a street in D.C. and spotted Edith

Opposite: Civilian
refugees from the
Picatinny explosion,
whose residences were
damaged or destroyed
by the explosion.

Above: Wilson speaking
to supporters at
his Shadow Lawn
campaign residence in
1916.

Right: Shadow Lawn
interior in 1916.

Patrick Tumulty, Wilson's chief of staff.

Galt on the sidewalk. He reportedly uttered the upper-class 1915 version of "she's a hottie" and subsequently married her.

Edith shared the caretaking of the president with his "private secretary" (today's chief of staff), Jersey City attorney Joseph Tumulty. Edith and Tumulty detested each other but ran the country in Wilson's name, pretending that the president was in control. The Republicans won an overwhelming victory in the election of 1920, electing Warren Harding president and achieving an increased dominance over Congress, using the campaign slogan "a return to normalcy." The American people were having second thoughts about their participation in the world war, which appeared to many as fought merely to expand European power, and turned inward. As Professor Tyler Austin Harper recently expressed it, "The 1920s were also a period when the public—traumatized by a recent pandemic, a devastating world war and startling technological developments—was gripped by the conviction that humanity might soon shuffle off this mortal coil. The '20s were indeed roaring, but they were also reeling."[9]

While Wilson was confined to his bed, things were getting a bit chaotic in the country. Although America was frequently and accurately described as a nation of immigrants, apprehension regarding immigrants was also part of the country's tradition. Benjamin Franklin was disturbed about the Pennsylvania "Dutch" continuing to speak in their native German, as he was understandably concerned about the unifying characteristic of a common language to a new nation.

By the mid-nineteenth century, the unrestricted flow of immigrants into the country was presumed to be a cultural threat by many Americans. Anxiety regarding German and particularity Irish Catholic immigration in the 1850s was responsible for the creation of the Native American Party, popularly called the Know-Nothing Party because of the party members' reluctance to talk about their membership and policies. The ethnic and racial fears lasted throughout the century. Chinese railroad workers created cultural apprehension that culminated in the Chinese Exclusion Act, signed by President Garfield on May 6, 1882. The law blocked Chinese people from immigrating to the United States and Chinese people already here from applying for citizenship.

In the last two decades of the nineteenth and the first two of the twentieth centuries, a large number of eastern and southern European immigrants came to America. Since the principal port of entry was New York, where immigrants were processed through Castle Garden and later Ellis Island, within sight of New Jersey, and the latter actually within the state's boundary waters, many of them ended their journey to a new life in the Garden State, which was industrializing rapidly and in need of unskilled and semiskilled labor. In 1900, it was estimated that 50 percent of New Jerseyans were either immigrants or the children of immigrants.

The census of 1910 listed 26 percent of the New Jersey population as being born in another country, the highest number before or since. It had declined somewhat by 1920, but not by much. That year, 58 percent of immigrants in New Jersey resided in the northeastern counties of Essex, Hudson and Passaic, mostly in the industrial cities of Newark, Jersey City and Paterson. Immigrants were accused of taking American jobs by working for less money and by some of being part of a conspiratorial ring to convert the country to Catholicism. A recent study maintains that immigrants actually improve the economy for all and are no danger to job-seeking Americans, a situation recently seconded by Nobel Prize–winning economist Paul Krugman.[10]

Immigrants did take jobs, but they were new ones created by substantial growth, not the traditional occupations of New Jerseyans.[11] New Jersey had been a developing industrial state for many years, but according to one account, "the guns of Europe" of World War I were responsible for "the most

Castle Garden, the chief nineteenth-century immigrant reception site in New York.

intense industrialization in its history." The production of high explosives, textiles, steel and ships rocketed to new heights. The Bureau of Statistics reported that expansion in manufacturing was 400 percent greater in 1916 than in any preceding year. The chemical industry in New Jersey sprang up almost overnight. Six factories for the production of aniline, formerly imported from Germany, were set up within the state, the most important at Kearny. Another source claims that the state's overall industrial output "increased almost 300 percent between 1914 and 1919."[12] Immigrants filled the expanding need for workers and contributed in other ways as well. A brief survey of the American soldiers who died in World War I who were residents of Middlesex County revealed that out of a total of 201, 73 were foreign born.[13]

While most immigrants from eastern and southern Europe were escaping a dismal agrarian lifestyle or, in the case of Russian Jews, confinement to the "Pale of Settlement" and were subject to economic and social prejudice and periodic murderous pogroms, some were politically radical. Paterson was a particularly notable New Jersey city for labor activists, many of them skilled silk workers from northern Italy, who conducted a number of strikes. In 1900, Gaetano Bresci, an Italian immigrant silk weaver and anarchist from

Immigrants at Castle Garden in the 1880s.

Paterson who left his job at the Hamil and Booth Silk Mill and returned to Europe, shot and killed King Umberto of Italy with a revolver he bought in Paterson. Bresci was not executed for the murder, as Italy had abolished capital punishment in 1889. He was sentenced to life imprisonment but was found dead in his cell on May 22, 1901. It was officially reported that he had committed suicide, but many thought otherwise.[14]

The Russian revolution gave hope to the radicals and created an unrealistic fear of a Communist insurrection in the United States. In 1920, Attorney General A. Mitchell Palmer, with motivation provided by an anarchist exploding a bomb at his front door, had his subordinate, J. Edgar Hoover, conduct a massive series of raids, arresting thousands of people suspected as anarchists and Communists. They were primarily Italian and Jewish immigrants, and hundreds were deported for their radical beliefs. The radicals retaliated by detonating a series of bombs, most notably one on New York City's Wall Street. None of this activity encouraged the average American to be a fan of immigration.[15]

Ironically, one of the most prominent American Communists was journalist John Reed, who was born to a wealthy West Coast family and attended Harvard University. Reed has his place in New Jersey history as well as the national story. He was a prominent supporter of the 1913 Paterson silk strike and was arrested there for his radicalism. He went on to sponsor a pageant to fund the strikers in Madison Square Garden. A war correspondent in World War I, he was a witness to and supporter of the Bolshevik revolution in Russia, and his book *Ten Days that Shook the World* told

Above: Immigrants from Russia at Ellis Island reception site, the successor of Castle Garden, in 1914.

Left: Gaetano Bresci, the Paterson, New Jersey silk worker who assassinated the king of Italy in 1900.

Opposite: The aftermath of the Wall Street bombing of 1920.

the story of that struggle. Reed died in Moscow of typhus in 1920 and was buried there as a hero by the Kremlin wall, where he remains to this day.[16]

Perhaps the most significant and unpleasant American development of the post–World War I era was the revival of the Ku Klux Klan, sparked by the Confederate-sympathizing film *The Birth of a Nation*, which portrayed the original Klan as saviors of white women from lust-filled recently freed African Americans. This was considered accurate history by President Wilson. African American soldiers who had served in France were coming home and demanding their civil rights, taken from them by the post-Reconstruction Jim Crow legislation. The result was a number of lynchings, some of African American veterans in uniform, and several massive destructive riots by white people, most notably in Tulsa, Oklahoma, where a prosperous Black neighborhood was totally destroyed. The new Klan, which was a pyramid scheme–style moneymaking operation (President Grant had crushed the original version), expanded across the country from Atlanta, exploiting fear and hatred in every state.

A *Trenton Times* article informed the public that the new Klan, which was organizing secretly in the state's cities, "has been especially successful in Newark and Elizabeth" and had plans of opening a Trenton headquarters "soon." That intent evoked a rapid response from African American war

veterans of the American Legion's Mitchell Davis Post. In a letter to Mayor Frederick W. Donnelly, the members of the post declared that they would oppose any attempts to establish a Klan chapter in Trenton, as it would be "regrettable" since "there is at present no feeling between races such as the Ku Klux Klan might incite."

Trenton commissioner of public safety George P. Labarre was more forthright. He told a journalist that "if the [Klan] members do commit any acts tending to race war or such disturbances they may as well know that they will be sent to jail or shot down in cold blood, if necessary." In a calmer vein, Hudson County African American Republican politician George Cannon saw little need to be alarmed. Cannon thought the Klan a primarily southern organization and believed it "would not be likely to gain much strength in New Jersey." Dean William Pickens, field secretary of the NAACP, disagreed and argued a necessity for "undivided cooperation with the Catholic Church and all other agencies through which the terrible and un-American attempts of the Ku Klux Klan may and can be completely frustrated."[17]

Opposite: Journalist and Communist John Reed.

Above: A KKK song written by a New Jerseyan and published in New Jersey.

The Klan came to New Jersey in the early 1920s. Klan leaders in Atlanta told recruiters to emphasize the chief fears of people in a particular state, and so, while white supremacy was a given in New Jersey's hooded ranks, the Klan also emphasized the need for "real Americans" to unite and also oppose immigrants, Catholics and Jews. The message did not work that well in the state, although on a national level, a series of laws in 1921, 1925 and 1927 steadily reduced the number of immigrants, particularly those from southern and eastern Europe, with discriminatory quotas.[18]

Although there were a number of theatrical Klan events, especially in the stronghold of Monmouth County, New Jersey Klansmen who ventured into immigrant-dense Perth Amboy on a recruiting mission barely escaped with their lives in an anti-Klan riot. Unlike states such as Indiana, where the Klan essentially ran the government during the 1920s, most New Jersey politicians, both Democrat and Republican, shunned Klan support. A few local officeholders, including one state legislator, Basil Bruno of Long Branch, courted their votes. When Bruno ran for Monmouth County sheriff, however, he was soundly defeated. When New Jersey grand dragon Arthur Bell summoned all Republican candidates to a meeting at the Robert Treat Hotel in Newark to be tested on their "Americanism," none showed up.[19]

Under the state constitution of 1844, New Jersey governors were forbidden from running for consecutive terms, so Governor Edwards went on to become a United States senator from New Jersey, and his successor in Trenton was George Silzer. Silzer, a progressive Democrat who had served as a state senator from Middlesex County and ally of Woodrow Wilson during the latter's term as governor, was currently serving as a judge. He was described as the "wettest" Democrat candidate available and won his primary. Elected in 1922, he served as governor from 1923 to 1926. Frank Hague supported Silzer for governor in return for the Middlesex party's support of former governor Edwards for the Senate, although as governor, Silzer did not work closely with the Jersey City mayor.[20]

Although much of his agenda was blocked by a Republican legislature, Silzer did achieve

ROAD MAP of NEW JERSEY 10¢

SHOWING
PAVED ROADS
HIGHWAY NUMBERS
MILEAGE BETWEEN TOWNS
POLE MARKINGS
INDEX OF TOWNS
POPULATIONS

PUBLISHED BY
The Clason Map Co.
CHICAGO

Opposite: Road map book of New Jersey in the 1920s.

Left: New Jersey Democratic governor Silzer (*right*).

some significant projects, including the bridge across the Delaware River between Camden and Philadelphia and the Holland Tunnel. He also replaced political hacks in the state road commission with engineers and charged them with creating a modern state road system. His biography states that he "laid the physical infrastructure for much of the state's post–World War II development."[21]

In 1923, Governor Silzer made clear his opposition to the Ku Klux Klan. He and a number of other New Jersey government officials received a circular sent out by the Klan, referring to "mobs which have disrupted meetings staged by the organization in various parts of New Jersey." Silzer responded that it "is not my intention to honor anonymous communications." On another occasion, when speaking at a dinner in Atlantic City, Silzer said, "Of all the undemocratic and un-American organizations, the Ku Klux Klan is the worst."[22]

After his term, Silzer served as chairman of the New York Port Authority, where he was involved in the planning for what would become the George Washington Bridge and managed the groundbreaking ceremonies for the iconic span across the Hudson. When his term at the Authority ended, then governor A. Harry Moore did not reappoint Silzer, and he returned to the practice of law, representing such well-known people as Arthur Flegenheimer, aka Dutch Shultz, in a tax evasion case. He died of a heart attack on October 16, 1940.[23]

New Jersey politics also received national notice during the 1920s. As previously noted, the United States Senate voted against ratifying the Treaty of Versailles. Wilson's successor, Warren Harding, requested that Congress pass a separate peace resolution. Republican senator Philander Knox of Pennsylvania introduced one in the Senate, and Republican representative Stephen Porter of Pennsylvania introduced a slightly different resolution in the House of Representatives. The resolutions were reconciled, and both houses passed the Knox-Porter Agreement. President Harding, returning from a golf outing at the Somerset Hills Country Club on July 2, 1921, signed the Knox-Porter Joint Congressional Resolution, declaring hostilities at an end, at the home of New Jersey senator Joseph S. Frelinghuysen in Raritan Borough, New Jersey. A small plaque marks the spot today.

President Harding's national "normalcy" did not include his private life. An alleged serial womanizer, he impregnated a young admirer, Nan Britton. Britton delivered her baby, Elizabeth Ann, in Asbury Park, New Jersey, in 1919. With cooperating ghostwriter Paul Wendel, a shady attorney, she wrote a book about her affair with Harding, *The President's Daughter*, in 1927 and was subjected to much vitriol and defamation. In 2015, a DNA sample matched a member of the Harding extended family, proving Elizabeth's mother Nan's contention.[24]

Harding would not live to the end of his term, dying of a heart attack on August 2, 1923, although there were unfounded rumors throughout the decade that his wife poisoned him in revenge for his infidelities. Calvin Coolidge, his vice president and the former governor of Massachusetts, was vacationing at Plymouth Notch, the rural Vermont community where he was born, when he was awakened in the early morning of August 2, 1923, and advised that his father, a notary public, was going to swear him in as president of the United States.[25]

Vermont was still largely living in the recent past, with mostly dirt roads, little electricity and limited telephone service. "Silent Cal" Coolidge, an old-fashioned reserved and modest soul, would become chief executive

President Warren Harding signs the Knox-Porter Agreement in New Jersey during a break from his golf game, officially ending the war with Germany in 1920.

Nan Britton, President Harding's mistress, and their child.

of a nation in dramatic transition, in rural Vermont as well as the more rapidly changing New Jersey. Coolidge, who endorsed civil rights for African and Native Americans but did not engage in legislative attempts to secure them, supported government in synchrony with his character, quiet and undemanding. Though he was far from perfect, Coolidge was fortunate enough to lead the country through its transition and into a more prosperous era that, unfortunately, would crash under his successor.[26]

On a more local level, Mary Norton of Jersey City, who worked as a volunteer in several local social organizations, including a Red Cross workroom for women during World War I, attracted the attention of some influential people in politics, including Frank Hague. Hague was impressed by Norton's enthusiasm and fundraising skills and, as women's ability to vote became a reality in the new decade, recruited her into the state's Democratic Party in 1921. The mayor reportedly told Norton, "It's your duty to organize the women of Jersey City."[27]

Norton soon became the first New Jersey female Democratic city committee member and then, in 1923, was elected as the first Democratic

Above, left: President Calvin Coolidge. *Library of Congress*.

Above, right: Mary Norton of Jersey City, New Jersey's first woman in Congress and the first Democratic congresswoman.

Opposite: Governor A. Harry Moore of New Jersey and New York governor and Democratic presidential candidate Alfred E. Smith and their wives at a massive rally in Sea Girt in 1928.

woman freeholder (today a commissioner) in New Jersey on the Hudson County Board of Freeholders. Noting the rate of infant mortality in Jersey City, she successfully obtained board approval and funding for the construction of a maternity hospital in the city at county expense, a special project of "Boss" Hague and named after his mother, Margaret.

Norton, encouraged by Hague, ran for the Twelfth New Jersey District seat in the United States Congress in 1924 and won in a landslide with 62 percent of the vote, as the first female Democrat and first New Jersey woman to serve in Congress. Eager to get started, she went to Washington several months before her term began to investigate possible committee assignments.[28]

On a state level, Silzer's successor, A. Harry Moore, was a Jersey City Democrat and member of Frank Hague's inner circle. Moore would go on to serve three three-year terms. Since a governor could not succeed himself in an immediate second term under the constitution of 1844, Moore, including one interruption to serve a partial term as a United States senator before returning to the state to run again for governor, set a record for the years an individual served as governor of the state since 1844.

Moore and Hague were active on the national level as well as in state affairs. On August 25, 1928, a crowd of eighty thousand enthusiastic New Jersey Democrats attended a rally at the governor's summer home at the National Guard Training Center in Sea Girt, organized by the two. They cheered the party's presidential candidate, Al Smith, and sang his campaign song, "The Sidewalks of New York." Just up the road in Ocean Grove that day, evangelist Billy Sunday attacked Smith, saying, "I don't find fault with him just because he is a Catholic, but because he is a Tammanyite, a Catholic and a wet, as well as an ambassador of the forces of hell."[29]

Moore was actually a fairly conservative Democrat who largely got along with his Republican-dominated legislature. In his stint as a senator following his gubernatorial term, he was the only Democratic senator to vote against the Social Security law, although Frank Hague's desire to be his constituents' Social Security might have had a bearing on that vote. Although he and his wife had no children, Moore sympathized with disabled young people and held an annual "crippled children's day" at his summer Sea Girt residence. Jersey City's School for Crippled Children was named for him in 1931. It still exists today as a branch of Jersey City University named A. Harry Moore School and listed as a "laboratory school" for disabled students.

As the decade came to a close, Republicans, who had controlled the legislature but not had a governor in some time, took advantage of the public approval of the president's "Coolidge prosperity" that had swept the

Top: Evangelist preacher Billy Sunday, who held a service up the road in Ocean Grove when Smith was heralded in Sea Girt and attacked Smith, saying, "I don't find fault with him just because he is a Catholic, but because he is a Tammanyite, a Catholic and a wet, as well as an ambassador of the forces of hell."

Bottom: Governor A. Harry Moore with a disabled child. He raised money for sick children throughout his life.

nation and nominated Morgan Foster Larson, an engineering graduate of Cooper Union Institute, for governor to oppose Frank Hague's candidate, former Motor Vehicle commissioner William L. Dill.

Larson had entered politics as a Republican state senate candidate from Middlesex County in 1921. Although Middlesex was normally a Democratic stronghold, Larson was respected due to his knowledge of infrastructure as a civil engineer and rose to become senate president. Hague, with the mistaken idea that Larson would be the easiest candidate to beat, had his supporters cross party lines in the primary to vote for Larson. Larson, to Hague's dismay, won the gubernatorial election and was inaugurated in 1929.

In the state senate, Larson had pushed New Jersey policy in the same direction as Governor Silzer, with new roads and bridges in what was rapidly becoming an automobile age. He increased backing for the construction of the Outerbridge Crossing and the Goethals Bridge and produced and passed a comprehensive and professional plan for the state's highway future. In his last days as governor, Larson cooperated with New York governor Franklin D. Roosevelt in the creation of the Lincoln Tunnel project.[30]

Despite his expertise, Larson's term was a failure for Republicans on several fronts. Although the Republicans controlled both houses of the legislature, Larson was more of an independent than a loyal party man and made appointments that were not approved by party leaders. Since the legislature was considerably more powerful than the governor under the constitution of 1844, many of Larson's initiatives and appointments failed. And then the economy collapsed with the stock market crash in October 1929. Larson also had personal problems. His wife, Jeanine, died, and he then married her secretary, Adda Schmidt. A plane crashed into his summer home in Sea Girt, narrowly missing his mother. His brothers were killed in an automobile accident, and he adopted their children. Larson left office in 1932, succeeded by A. Harry Moore, who returned for his second term.[31]

New Jersey governor Foster Larson (*right*) and New York governor Herbert Lehman at the George Washington Bridge cable-laying in 1929.

Left: Widowed New Jersey governor Foster Larson and his new bride in December 1930.

Below: A plane crashed into the governor's summer home at Sea Girt. *National Guard and Milita Museum of New Jersey.*

Governor Edward Edwards, who began the decade as New Jersey's chief executive and went on to serve as one of New Jersey's United States senators, lost his Senate reelection bid to Republican Hamilton Fish Kean. Edwards's wife died in 1928 and he lost most of his money in the stock market crash of 1929. He had a dispute with Mayor Hague that ended his political career and then found out he had cancer. On January 26, 1931, after making sure his pet parrot had sufficient food and water, Edwards went into the bedroom of his apartment at 181 Kensington Avenue in Jersey City, laid down on the bed and shot himself in his head. His decade died with him.[32]

Chapter 2

PROHIBITION

A s noted in the previous chapter, New Jersey gubernatorial candidate Edward Edwards promised to keep New Jersey as "wet as the Atlantic Ocean" despite the impending federal imposition of Prohibition with ratification of the Eighteenth Amendment on January 16, 1919, with a ban on alcohol sales due to begin nationwide at midnight, January 17, 1920.

To be fair, Edwards did try some legal ways to limit the amendment's force in New Jersey, one of three states that had not yet ratified the Eighteenth Amendment, by legalizing beer at 3.5 or 2.5 percent of alcohol and by instructing his attorney general to initiate lawsuits challenging the constitutionality of the amendment, but they did not pass legal muster. Nevertheless, bootleggers and rumrunners quickly went to work as the demand was high and the profits huge—and the state was pretty wet. Nationwide, Republicans were more supportive of Prohibition than Democrats. In New Jersey, however, many in both parties opposed the idea. Bootlegging production and illegal importation of alcoholic beverages flourished across the state for the next decade.[33]

The prohibition movement had a long history in the United States and had gradually strengthened on local levels over the years. It became a common cause for a lot of suffragists along with women's ability to vote, as they had witnessed husbands spending their pay in taverns rather than bringing it home to help their families. In 1890, Congress banned the sale of "intoxicating beverages" to enlisted military personnel at posts in states or counties with local prohibition laws. The military did not extend the ban to beer, as it was considered less dangerous, and beer sales could be approved on post by local commanders.

Down to the present day, soldiers have loved their beer. German immigrant Otto Scheu, the great-great-uncle of coauthor Harry Ziegler, served in the United States Army as a career soldier in the final decade of the nineteenth century and in the first decade of the twentieth and fought in Cuba and the Philippines. During the twenty-five years he served, Scheu was reduced in rank several times for excessive alcohol consumption, and once, after being discharged for the end of an enlistment period and swearing never to return to the army, he and another veteran tore up a bar in New York City.

Otto Scheu, a German immigrant who became a career soldier in the American army, engaged in a few drunken brawls around the close of the nineteenth century.

The judge offered them jail or reenlistment. They chose the latter.[34]

Congress expanded its military prohibition law in the Canteen Act of 1901, which prohibited "the sale of, or dealing in, beer, wine or any intoxicating liquors by any person in any post exchange or canteen or army transport or upon any premises used for military purposes by the United States." The definition of "intoxicating beverages" contained a loophole, as the law specified permission to consume beverages containing a vague and undetermined "appreciative quantity of alcohol" upon permission from local civilian authorities.

When America entered World War I, Congress extended alcohol prohibition beyond military post boundaries, ostensibly, according to some, to preserve grain for wartime use but perhaps more likely as part of a growing moral imperative. The Selective Service Act of 1917 prohibited the sale or consumption of intoxicating beverages in a five-mile-wide zone around each post. The same law made it illegal to sell intoxicating beverages to a member of the armed forces in uniform anywhere; the Judge Advocate General's Office in 1918 defined intoxicants as containing 1.4 percent or more alcohol.

During World War I, Hoboken, New Jersey, became a military town, due to its designation as a port of exit for France for the large number of men who traveled through nearby Camp Merritt. Soldiers patrolled the streets on the lookout for enemy sympathizers among the city's large German American population. In addition, the army, obeying the recent legislation and incidentally setting the stage for postwar prohibition, banned the sale of alcohol to soldiers and demanded that local saloons surrounding the embarkation piers be closed so that soldiers were not tempted to have a parting glass before boarding ships for the war. Federal authorities then upped the ante by insisting that taverns within a half-mile radius of the docks be shut down and that those beyond that distance close by 10:00 p.m. every night. The city fathers resisted these last demands, allowing bars to stay open well past the designated hour. Eventually, a compromise was reached, but by then, many of Hoboken's traditional watering holes had closed due to loss of business.

Along with military police, agents of the Federal Bureau of Investigation patrolled Hoboken, on the alert for imbibing soldiers as well as German sympathizers and draft evaders. The agents, and their volunteer vigilante assistants, also kept watch on other military installations and their surrounding towns across the state, including Camps Dix, Merritt and Alfred Vail. Not satisfied with investigating the drinking habits of soldiers in federal service, agents visited Camp Edge at Sea Girt, New Jersey, in August 1917 as a result of "several complaints that the militia now encamped at Sea Girt were obtaining liquors and bringing them on the encampment." Two investigators patrolled the camp, saw no obvious drunks and spoke to several officers, who professed ignorance of the matter and suggested that if any alcohol did enter the camp gates, it was obtained in "Manasquan or Belmar."[35]

Mirroring the military experience, civilian prohibition movements gained strength during the first two decades of the twentieth century as well. In 1915, the Anti-Saloon League held its national convention in Atlantic City, New Jersey, between June 6 and 9. Founded in Ohio in 1893, the Anti-Saloon League became the "most effective organization of the temperance forces of the United States" after going national in 1895. The League agitated for prohibition of alcohol sales on a state and local level with a good deal of success, and a contemporary source noted that "by January 1916, half the population and seventy-one percent of the area of the United States will be legally dry."

The League members who gathered that summer in Atlantic City had much to be proud of, as their goal of "the extermination of the beverage liquor traffic" on a national level seemed well within reach. The convention was described as a sort of combination political rally and religious revival.

ON LIBERTY
IN
HOBOKEN, N. J.

Mayor Griffin—Dr. Stuckey

War Camp Community Service, Hoboken Branch
Headquarters, Room 17, No. 1 Newark Street

Above: A pamphlet composed by city officials in Hoboken to give to soldiers, providing them possible alternatives to drinking. Hoboken was a major point of departure of American soldiers, and many spent their spare time seeking open bars.

Following: Members of the Anti-Saloon League pose on the beach at their 1916 convention at Atlantic City.

Saloon League of America
In July 6-9, 1915.

Although the organization claimed to be nonpartisan, the membership was composed mostly of Protestant Republicans, including many ministers, although a Catholic priest from Pennsylvania addressed the conventioneers and endorsed their goals.

As we all know in retrospect, the Anti-Saloon League's eventual triumph did not produce its long-term expected results, which was something the confident convention delegates could no doubt not conceive of when they posed for a celebratory photo on the Atlantic City Beach in that summer of 1915.

On January 17, 1920, the Volstead Act, the law enforcing the dictates of the recently approved Eighteenth Amendment to the Constitution, went into effect, prohibiting the commercial sale of alcoholic beverages and enforcing the "noble experiment" reformers in the League had been pushing on an alcohol-sodden public for a number of years. There were exceptions. Section 29 of the Volstead Act initially allowed homeowners to produce two hundred gallons of "non-intoxicating cider and fruit juice" a year. The maximum allowed alcohol level, a 0.5 percent, was, however, dropped, allowing amateur vintners to produce alcoholic wine, as long as it was "consumed in domiciles" or religious services. There was a subsequent tenfold increase in home winemaking over the decade. Wine was made from both "wine bricks," which were boxes of concentrated grapes, and actual grapes. Grape growers, mostly from California, shipped both products nationwide. By the autumn of 1928, it was estimated that one thousand railroad cars loaded with "wine stuff" would arrive by railroad in Newark, New Jersey, described as "the center of the grape receiving area."

Although already manufactured alcohol was quickly concealed and available for the first year of postwar Prohibition, as supplies were consumed, bootleggers and rumrunners became the primary providers selling banned beverages. They violated the Prohibition law in New Jersey in different ways, although some individuals participated in both practices. As a coastal state lacking enthusiasm for the Volstead Act, New Jersey was a prime destination for rumrunners, who used small craft to "run" out beyond the three-mile limit in the Atlantic Ocean, load up with legally produced alcohol from other countries and then bring it back ashore. Although there were rumrunner ports up and down both coasts, in New Jersey the most well-known areas were Atlantic City, where Republican political boss Enoch "Nucky" Johnson was amenable to looking the other way on different aspects of illegal activity if sufficiently compensated, and the Bayshore area of northern Monmouth County, where local authorities

Two young ladies sample the wine grapes transported from California to Newark, New Jersey. Under the Prohibition law, individuals were allowed to make wine for their own use or religious ceremonies.

accepted protection money from the runners and there was easy access to densely populated urban areas.

In peacetime, the Coast Guard serves under the aegis of the Treasury Department, so in August 1922, it was treasury secretary Andrew Mellon who ordered Coast Guard cutters to assemble at Cape May, New Jersey, for "a training period of war maneuvers and target practice." Although some thought the exercise was initiated as preparation for pursuing rumrunners, Mellon explained that the "mobilization was ordered to keep the personnel in trim for prompt transfer to the fighting line of the navy in the event of another war."

The training assignment involved eight vessels and six hundred officers and men and included a stint of "infantry battalion drill" ashore, as well as sea maneuvers over the ten-day period. Races between ten oared lifeboats, sailboats and motorboats became tourist events that drew large crowds to the shore. In the end, the cutter *Modoc* was "decorated the most efficient

Opposite: Unloading liquor from a large ship at sea into a smaller rumrunner boat on its way to the Jersey shore.

Left: Al Capone (*fourth from left*) strides along the Atlantic City boardwalk in the 1920s. Nucky Johnson appears on his left. While Al and Nucky knew each other, this photo seems an early attempt at Photoshopping.

ship" overall, and the crew was presented with a large cup to represent their overall win.

A suspected rumrunner appeared early on in Atlantic City. Federal government agents thought they had solved the mystery of an "elusive pirate ship" that had been spotted at "various times off the New Jersey coast, near Montauk Point and in Long Island Sound," when they raided the *Pokomoke*, docked in Gardner's Basin in the inlet section of Atlantic City, on July 23, 1921.

The *Pokomoke* had set out from Nassau in the Bahamas, allegedly bound for Canada with a load of liquor, and local rumor had it that the booze had instead been delivered to the New Jersey resort city by the sea, no doubt with the approval of "Nucky" Johnson.

Although the schooner's manifest detailed its alcohol cargo, there was no contraband booze on the *Pokomoke* at the time it was seized. The captain, Canadian J.A. Roy, explained that his ship had sprung a leak off the New Jersey coast on its way to Canada and that in order to save it from sinking, he had thrown the thousand cases of liquor he was transporting overboard and then sailed in to Atlantic City for repairs.

No one believed the story, of course, and there was no evidence of a leak in the boat's hull. While Coast Guardsmen took possession of the *Pokomoke*, federal Prohibition agents "combed Atlantic City for a trace of Captain Roy's cargo." Unsurprisingly, there is no evidence that they ever found it. It was a successful rum run. A newspaper article several years later identified the *Pokomoke* crew as composed of "many prominent residents of the shore city."[36]

Prohibition violations were often used to provide publicity for other groups. Arthur Bell, New Jersey grand dragon of the revived Ku Klux Klan, designed to attract Americans distraught at the social changes of

Top: Crew of the *Modoc*, displaying its trophy at a Coast Guard station at Cape May, New Jersey.

Bottom: The rumrunner *Pokomoke* docked in Atlantic City, New Jersey.

the post–World War I world, apparently perceived the Monmouth County communities along Raritan Bay's Bayshore beaches as a region with much Klan potential. In early January 1924, there was a Klan meeting at Highlands Methodist Church in the Bayshore community of Atlantic Highlands. About one hundred costumed Klansmen attended the gathering, with an estimated seven hundred curious residents gathering inside and outside of the church.

Atlantic Highlands, New Jersey, in the 1920s.

Bell, accompanied by his wife, Leah, promised, in his self-righteous style, to "clean up the bootleg business" along the bay. The implied threat of vigilante action had by now become a staple of the Klan's "public service" announcements. Following Bell's opening address, Belmar Klan leader J.B. Baker advised the audience that "we know the conditions here. We know the rum-runners and Boot Leggers are buying politicians. We are going to see that this is cleaned up."[37]

The Bayshore was indeed a problematic area. The region's attraction as a tourist destination as well as a commercial fishing mecca had been seriously degraded by raw sewage that, combined with other residue drifting down from the cities to the north, particularly New York, had substantially spoiled some areas of a once charming district. Oil slicks and debris turned one section of the Bayshore into an area known as the "mud hole," and the stench from rotting garbage and dead animals along certain beaches was horrendous. The environmental degradation had cost jobs, but as the saying goes, nature abhors a vacuum.

Prohibition provided new employment and business opportunities, and the Bayshore became a major smuggling point for the importation and distribution of alcoholic beverages, increasingly funded by wealthy New York gangsters like Arnold Rothstein. As Prohibition continued, the gangsters became the overall financial managers of the smuggling. Liquor-laden ships anchored offshore at "rum row," beyond the international three-mile limit, and runners sailed their smaller craft out to load liquor and run it back to shore, primarily at Atlantic Highlands, although cargoes landed all along the Bayshore as opportunities arose. The captains reportedly received five dollars (eighty-five dollars in 2023 money) per run, and the laborers

Cape May Coast Guard crew training for its mission—catching rumrunners.

unloading the boats were paid one dollar (seventeen dollars) for their work and another one dollar for loading the smuggled alcohol onto trucks that whisked it away for distribution.[38]

Many organized crime leaders who assumed leadership in the rumrunning trade, including mobsters Al Lillien and Vito Genovese, were Jewish or Italian immigrants or sons of immigrants, as were the hijackers the illegal liquor trade attracted to Bayshore communities to steal landed liquor. It was a way for them to climb the economic ladder.

Gunfights erupted between rumrunners and hijackers across the Bayshore. Rival gangs increasingly exchanged gunfire in the streets of Atlantic Highlands, where law enforcement was thwarted by local officials, including the Atlantic Highlands chief of police, John Snedeker, who was believed to be on the mob payroll.

On October 20, 1923, a gun battle between bootleggers and gangsters from Newark over possession of a shipment of smuggled liquor erupted in the streets of Atlantic Highlands. One man, Frank LeConte of Newark, was mortally wounded and several others injured as local residents dove for cover. Several men were arrested, but no one on either side of the dispute would testify, so all charges were dropped.[39]

In many ways, Bell's "clean up" pledge was a joke. For Klansmen to hint at taking matters into their own hands as vigilantes was pretty much a work of fiction, in the same vein as Bell's promises to help solve murders around the state. Vigilantism had been roundly condemned by New Jersey public officials, from the governor on down, and frankly, the state's working- and middle-class Protestant Bible-spouting Klan membership was a poor match for murderous gangsters armed with Thompson submachine guns. Although they were involved in police and vigilante actions in other states, particularly Indiana, where Klan-confiscated liquor mysteriously disappeared, and in the South, there is no evidence of the Ku Klux Klan either aiding law enforcement or acting as a private police force in New Jersey to any extent.[40]

The Klan was a joke, but the Coast Guard appeared to be a more serious remedy for rumrunning. "Rumrunners beware! Coast Guardsmen from the Cape May station are ready for you!" At least that is the message the Coast Guard hoped to convey with a photo released to the newspapers in December 1921. The caption reads: "One-pounders and machine guns are ready to stem the tide of Christmas liquor when the attempt is made to smuggle it through the blockade by Rum Runners for holiday consumption. Here is one of the patrol boats from the base at Cape May, N.J. ready for action." It is safe to assume that success in stemming the tide of "Christmas liquor" was minimal and that the Guardsmen in the photo may have sampled a cocktail or two themselves over the holidays. In fact, a newspaper report from 1925 detailed the court-martial conviction of six Coast Guardsmen who were also running rum.[41]

By the middle of the decade, rumrunners appear to have achieved a bit of social acceptance and reportedly responded to stories of an imminent federal crackdown on rumrunning in Highlands "with a broad grin." They certainly did not hide from journalists. The *Asbury Park Press* headlined in December 1923 that "twice as much liquor has landed as last year they say—20 ships along row with cheer for New Year's." Interviewed runners denied rumors that they were also smuggling drugs and illegal Chinese immigrant laborers into New Jersey coastal towns, tales no doubt spread to turn local citizens against them. While the center of the trade was in the Bayshore, landings were also reported in Asbury Park, Point Pleasant and even the Methodist religious stronghold of Ocean Grove. The runners concluded the interview by "saying they had a 'Merry Christmas' and displaying a large wad of bills" to back their claims.[42]

Newspapers actually published the names of prominent rumrunners, including Angelo Bargellarmo, "one of the shrewdest Rum Runners in the

Aerial view of a rumrunner heading for the Jersey shore.

business"; Eddie Cogvill, whose "fleet of five speedboats are streaming out to sea like the ships of the Atlantic fleet in battle formation"; and Hughey Thompson, "whose hand was on the tiller of the fastest rum running boat in the business" operating out of Highlands.[43]

Although some small craft were captured by the Coast Guard, most were apparently able to easily penetrate the guard's "rum run blockade," reach ships waiting to unload imported foreign brand name liquor and successfully return with their cargo. In 1925, a news photographer went along for a rumrunner ride off the Jersey coast and took a photo of liquor being loaded onto the runner boat, reporting that the crew made "two runs to the Jersey shore with him aboard" and ended the night attending a dance on one of the large ships. He described the runner crew as "college bred, most of them of gentlemanly mien but daredevil swashbuckling lads" who "didn't consider their trade criminal," perhaps as a contrast to immigrant gangster rumrunners and native hillbilly bootleggers operating urban and rural stills.[44]

It wasn't all partying. Rumrunning, or even being in a boat in the water near the Bayshore in the 1920s, was dangerous. Gerard Kadenbach, a twenty-four-year-old local resident, was alone in his boat in July 1924 when a Coast Guard cutter approached and a crewman shot him. No liquor was found on board his boat, and it was not clear whether he had dumped it into the ocean at the sight of the Coast Guard (a not uncommon practice) or there had never been any liquor on board. Kadenbach was taken to a hospital in Long Branch, where he died. A Monmouth County investigation into the matter was cancelled by a local Coast Guard superintendent, who maintained that the investigation was a federal responsibility. There was none.[45]

New Jersey and federal Prohibition enforcement authorities were more likely to pursue local bootleggers who produced beer and alcohol in the state than rumrunners who imported it. On March 17, 1922, the Hobart Act, New Jersey's implementation law for the Eighteenth Amendment, was passed by the state legislature. George Hobart, New Jersey assembly speaker in 1921, was the sponsor of the law, which was initially vetoed by Governor Edwards but passed over his veto by the Republican legislature. It criminalized the possession as well as production of alcoholic beverages, and arrests were often for minor offenses. In the year ending June 30, 1923, 982 people were arrested in Atlantic City under the Hobart Act simply for being drunk.[46]

Initial arrests under this law and the federal Volstead Act for actual bootlegging numbered 91 in 1922 but, by 1932, had escalated to 996. There was a total of 4,768 arrests for manufacturing, sale, possession and transportation of alcohol in New Jersey during Prohibition, about 400 of them for traditional "Jersey Lightning" or "applejack," most of the latter in Sussex, Warren and Hunterdon Counties.

Prohibition had a major impact on many small New Jersey businesses, where owners suddenly found themselves on the wrong side of the Volstead and Hobart laws. George F. Grause of Red Bank, the son of German immigrants, was granted a license to produce beer in 1919 but was forced to relinquish his license a year later. The Volstead Act forced the closure of Grause's small brewing company, and he had to sell his bottling equipment for a fraction of what he had paid for it. Unsurprisingly, Grause, who had years of experience in the legal bottling business, succumbed to the temptation of the illegal alcohol trade and in 1924 was arrested in a raid in Monmouth County's town of Red Bank for selling liquor. Following the repeal of Prohibition, Grause's application for a liquor license in Red Bank was denied, perhaps due to his previous conviction.[47]

Other small bootleggers were more fortunate. James M. Maher, a descendent of Irish immigrants, was a farmer in Holmdel and knew how to convert apple cider into "Jersey Lightning." He built a new home in 1923 and installed a 330-gallon whiskey still in the attic. The house also had a horseshoe driveway that looped around it and protected customers from being seen purchasing his product at the back door. He was never arrested and operated his entrepreneurial business until Prohibition ended in 1933. He later served as Holmdel's fire chief.[48]

Some obvious bootleggers were blatantly exonerated by local juries. In 1930, farmer John Krapka of Upper Freehold Township was arrested for illegal manufacturing and possession of liquor. It was charged that he "unlawfully manufactured and cause[d] to be manufactured certain spirituous, vinous, malt and brewed liquors, intoxicating and fit for the use for beverage purposes." When his case came to trial, Krapka claimed that he had rented his barn to two men and, unlikely as it seemed, had no idea what they were doing on the premises. He was acquitted.[49]

Some federal officials, however, did their best to stanch the flow of illegal booze across the state, and sometimes they were successful, at least temporarily. During a January 11, 1929 raid in Hoboken, they arrested Walter Webber of Jersey City, Richard Smith of Manhattan and Charles Barone of Brooklyn. The trio were hauled before United States commissioner Edward R. Stanton and charged with "operating an unlicensed still."

While the perpetrators cooled their heels in jail, unable to make the $2,500 bail, federal agents destroyed their "$25,000 worth of distillery apparatus." The still had churned out 500 gallons of raw whiskey a day. When production ceased, there were "300 drums containing 50 gallons each of alcohol and 50 cases containing 24-gallon cans of alcohol" stored in the building.

Bootlegging could be a dangerous enterprise aside from legal difficulties. A massive explosion "shook the countryside for miles around" Woodstown, New Jersey, on December 2, 1931, and sent a three-ton boiler through the wall of a barn and flying off through the air. The boiler hit the nearby farmhouse of Fred Danner, driving a ten-foot-wide hole through the home before it landed in a field. Local firemen and citizens quickly put out the fire the explosion had started in the barn. The boiler had been a component of a liquor-making still, and state police later reported that "the still was an elaborate affair, made for large scale production."

Danner, his wife and their seven children were tossed out of bed when the boiler hit their house, and the children were struck with debris as it passed in front of their bedrooms. Fortunately, they were only slightly injured. The same was not true for the men tending the still, which had a ten-thousand-gallon capacity. Both were killed, and one of them was tossed 450 feet away

A bootlegger still in Hoboken.

from the barn. They were "mangled beyond recognition" and remained unidentified. Authorities had little to work with. One corpse had a gold ring marked "R.G.," and there were some "laundry marks" on their clothing. Woodstown police chief William Pennel posited that the boiler "probably

Results of the still explosion in Woodstown, New Jersey, in 1931. The still hurtled through the air and blew a ten-foot hole in the farmhouse.

went dry with an exceedingly hot fire under it and the accumulated heat caused the explosion."

Prohibition agents from Camden arrested Danner and told reporters they might charge him with manslaughter due to the deaths. He, in turn, said that the two men to whom he had leased the barn, who had not given him their names, said they were going to make tallow in the building and that he had no idea they were distilling alcohol. He was subsequently released.

There were other explosions as well, not necessarily due to accidents. In March 1931, as Prohibition agents began to dismantle a one-thousand-gallon capacity liquor still in the 1 Vermont Avenue home of the Brancolini family in Lawrence Township, it exploded, seriously injuring five of the agents and three hired "wreckers." Trenton firemen called to the scene expressed the view that the explosion was the result of "a bomb left in the building."

In 1926, Ira L. Reeves was appointed to take charge of the New Jersey Federal Prohibition office, located in Newark. Reeves was widely respected due to his heroism as an officer in World War I, when he was wounded and cited for bravery and promoted, and his postwar presidency of Norwich

The Woodstown still ended up in a field.

University, a military school in Vermont. Reeves was a firm believer in Prohibition and ordered his agents to increase raids across the state on all illegal operations, from speakeasy saloons to stills and breweries.

Reeves refused bribes and ignored angry protesters of his administration in his attempt to make New Jersey completely dry. He failed and discovered that many of his agents were accepting bribes that exceeded their salaries. He quit after eight months on the job and gave speeches and wrote articles about how Prohibition had failed, summing up his experience in a 1931 book, *Ol' Rum River: Revelations of a Prohibition Administrator*. Reeves went on to become western director of the Crusaders, an anti-Prohibition organization, and debated William Upshaw, a Prohibitionist candidate for president.[50]

On March 20, 1930, "a squad of Prohibition agents armed with pistols, shotguns, axes and heavy trucks which were used as battering rams raided the Hensler brewery in Newark and confiscated some seven thousand barrels of beer. The Boot Leggers who were running the place had a pipe line running under the street from the brewery to an old garage where they filled their barrels with the banned beverage at the rate of five barrels at a clip." The

Colonel Reeves (*right*) and Mr. Upshaw agree to debate Prohibition.

garage was owned by one T.B. Plunkett, who later claimed ignorance of the beer line into his property, a claim a judge would later dismiss.

The raid was led by New York based Captain George E. "Hard Boiled" Golding, the "ace of undercover men in the Prohibition service," who was known for employing "rough house and strong-arm methods in enforcing the dry law." In 1951, a Chicago reporter remembered that Golding had come to town in 1928 with an entourage of thirty agents, "most of them young and untrained," some of whom "seemed overeager to use the submachine guns with which they were equipped." After several raids, during which Golding's trigger-happy agents shot several citizens, including an insurance agent who happened to be walking by, and even raided a police station where a janitor had smuggled a bottle of bourbon to a prisoner, Golding was transferred, allegedly at the request of a U.S. senator, to Baltimore.

If Golding learned anything from his Chicago experience, it did not seem to stick. By 1930, as leader of a special detachment, he apparently had carte blanche to travel around the country making raids but was a continued source of complaints filed by citizens and local law enforcement. One

The building across the street from the Hensler brewery, where beer was pumped for illegal distribution.

Prohibition agents dumping captured beer into the street.

journalist writing about the Newark operation noted that Golding "popped up one day with a dozen agents armed like cowboys and raided the Hensler brewery, getting 7,000 barrels of beer—the largest single seizure in Jersey. It was done without the aid or knowledge of the regular Prohibition unit stationed in that territory." In addition to confiscating the beer, Golding's team arrested thirty-six men and women on the premises of the brewery and garage. Within a short period, the brewery was back in covert action under the name of Superior Manufacturing Company, however, and was raided once again in November 1931.

The Hensler Brewery, founded by Joseph Hensler in 1860, was one of twenty-seven legal breweries that once called Newark home. It occupied a large building at 73 Wilson Avenue in the Down Neck or Ironbound section of the city. Wilson Avenue was formerly known as Hamburg Place but was renamed during the anti-German hysteria of World War I.

With the advent of Prohibition, breweries across the nation had closed. Some quickly reopened, however, "repurposed" to blend more innocuous beverages like "near beer" or soda or as icehouses and similar businesses. For some, however, as with Hensler, that new life was merely a mask for the continued production of beer. The Hensler brewery reopened legally at the end of Prohibition in 1933 and produced what the company advertising staff dubbed as "A Whale of a Beer," with a publicity truck representing a whale, until it closed in 1958.

And Captain Golding? Oh yes. In July 1930, Golding was "relieved of his duties" as a result of "charges being filed with Washington by a young woman," who turned out to be "a stenographer in Golding's office." He was dismissed in November, but the bureau never revealed the exact reason. One can guess.

In the aftermath of the stock market crash of 1929, influential industrialists and Wall Street bankers, who initially supported Prohibition as a remedy to solve the perceived problem of drunken and hence less productive workers, began to change their perspective. When Prohibition was initiated, it caused a significant drop in government revenue through loss of federal taxes, some say up to $11 billion over the next decade. Concerned that the deepening Depression caused a nosedive in federal revenue that might result in an increase in their taxes, these wealthy men began to quietly lobby for the end of Prohibition and the return of alcohol excise tax revenue to the treasury.

Prohibition was beginning to crumble. The September 28, 1931 meeting of New Jersey Republican legislators and leaders, never overwhelming fans of Prohibition, at the Robert Treat Hotel in Newark was called

New Jersey Republican congressman Fred Hartley of Kearny threw a bipartisan party at the Club Michel in Washington, D.C., on April 7, 1933, to "celebrate the return of beer."

to draft "a proposal for the legalization of 4% beer to be submitted to President Hoover." In the presidential election of 1932, Franklin D. Roosevelt campaigned on a promise to push for repeal of Prohibition and proclaimed it at a Frank Hague–produced massive rally at Sea Girt. Once in office, Roosevelt signed a law legalizing beer, and on December 5, 1933, the Eighteenth Amendment was formally repealed with the passage of the Twenty-First Amendment to the Constitution.

New Jersey Republican representative Fred Hartley of Kearny threw a bipartisan party at the Club Michel in Washington, D.C., on April 7, 1933, to "celebrate the return of beer" following Roosevelt's signing of the Cullen-Harrison Act, which amended the 1920 Volstead Act to allow the production of 3.2 percent beer and "light wines." Hartley was photographed with Democrats John J. Delaney of New York and Patrick J. Boland and Francis E. Walter of Pennsylvania. Hartley and Walter appeared to have had more than a few.

Jersey was legally wet once more!

Chapter 3

CULTURE AND ENTERTAINMENT

There was vast cultural change, in the nation and world as well as in New Jersey, in the 1920s, an era that gained a few enduring nicknames, most notably the Roaring Twenties. The term "Jazz Age" received a big boost by American novelist F. Scott Fitzgerald's short story collection, *Tales of the Jazz Age*, published by Charles Scribner's Sons in September 1922. A hodge-podge of different literary styles and themes, the book was analogous to the era.

As the term "Jazz Age," which some say was actually coined by Fitzgerald, implies, a new style of popular music was an important aspect of 1920s entertainment and culture as its influence was expanded by advances in recording and radio. Jazz had its roots in New Orleans African American music. There is probably no more well-known person with New Jersey origins connected to jazz between the world wars than William "Count" Basie. Born in Red Bank in 1904 to William and Lily Ann Basie, he started playing piano in his childhood years with instruction from his mother and then a professional piano teacher.

Basie had a natural ear for popular music and, as an adolescent, performed odd jobs at Red Bank's Palace Theatre and filled in for the venue's piano player when he was unavailable, providing accompaniment to silent films and vaudeville performances. In the 1920s, Basie formed a small jazz band and started playing in speakeasy illegal taverns in Red Bank and Asbury Park. In January 1921, he "won a prize of $2.50 in gold" at a piano-playing contest in Asbury Park. In 1924, he and a bandmate moved to Harlem in

Red Bank, New Jersey's musical genius, "Count" Basie, with his band in Chicago.

New York City, then the center of African American culture, literature and music. From there, Basie scaled the music heights, becoming a nationally recognized master of jazz in the 1920s and swing music in the succeeding decade. But it all began in New Jersey. And so, we titled our book to honor the musical genius from Red Bank—Count Basie.

In the 1920s, the role of women in society became far more significant, and formerly downplayed or hidden behavior became relevant or significant—or entertaining. The end of World War I and the independence some women had achieved by war work during its course, coupled with their ability to vote, the rise of jazz music, films and more revealing clothing, led to a new world. One of these changes was the rise of the beauty pageant, in which Atlantic City, New Jersey, played a major role. In September 1920, the city's "fall frolic," intended to attract business after the end of summer, involved several hundred "young maidens" seated in wicker rolling chairs pushed down the boardwalk in a parade that attracted several hundred observers. The city's Businessmen's League decided to expand it the following year.[51]

For several years, newspapers around the country had sponsored beauty pageants that made ranking decisions based on photographs submitted by young women. The Atlantic City sponsors decided to do it live and asked newspapers across the Northeast to submit contestants whose journey to the city by the sea would be funded by the city's businessmen. Nine young women appeared in the first "intercity beauty contest," but more importantly, 100,000 tourists showed up, extending the city's profitable summer season into September. Although there were several prizes, the overall winner was sixteen-year-old Margaret Gorman, of Washington, D.C., who was dubbed "Miss America" by a local newspaper reporter, a title used by the sponsors in later years. But in 1921, she was declared the winner of the "Golden Mermaid" or "Bathers' Review" competition and garnered a $100 prize. As an additional attraction, the Atlantic City sponsors recruited explosives inventor Hudson Maxim, who resided in New Jersey, with laboratories in Farmingdale and Lake Hopatcong, to portray King Neptune.[52]

The pageant caught the attention of Oklahoma congressman Manuel Herrick, who was appalled by beauty contests as "a peril to the nation." Herrick proposed legislation that would put an end to pageants "before the much-discussed American girl 'drifts further afield from home.'" Herrick

Opposite: Atlantic City's Fall Frolic of 1920, designed to bring tourists to the city after the summer season.

Right: Margaret Gorman, winner of the 1921 Bathers' Review who was retroactively declared the first Miss America.

Below: Hudson Maxim, explosive and gunpowder inventor who lived at Lake Hopatcong, New Jersey, was recruited to play King Neptune in 1921, with Margaret Gorman by his side.

went on to blame newspapers for the "insidious and demoralizing" contests. His proposed legislation, which of course did not pass, provided that "it shall be unlawful for any newspaper or advertising agency to hold any beauty contest contrary to this act or any contest wherein any moving picture company or film producer or theatrical Company are allowed to participate therein. Violation of the law shall be punishable by a fine of $5,000, imprisonment for one year, or both."[53]

Herrick, a self-educated one-term congressman and self-ordained preacher, was certainly out of step with much of America. His mother was sure he was the second coming of Jesus, a conclusion he largely shared. After robbing a train in his youth, he spent several years at an insane asylum. While in office, Herrick, also known as the "Okie Jesus," perhaps surprisingly, largely adhered to the party line and service to his constituents. As one account puts it, however, "his good work was overshadowed by his eccentricities and by his lack of knowledge of governmental processes."[54]

As time went by, some may have thought Herrick had a point. By 1923, the contest was known as the Atlantic City Beauty Pageant. Charlotte Isabel Nash was a contestant that year as Miss Saint Louis, and she came close to winning. One of the judges, forty-five-year-old Philadelphia and Atlantic City theater mogul Fred Nixon-Nirdlinger, became smitten with the eighteen-year-old Charlotte and proposed marriage. She accepted, and after completing a course at a finishing school where Nirdlinger sent her to smooth her rough edges, they were married in Hagerstown, Maryland, on February 3, 1924.

Nirdlinger had a checkered romantic past. His first marriage, to actress Tessie Burke, with whom he had two sons, had ended in divorce in 1908. He married again, to Lura McKenna, in 1909, but when and where that marriage ended was rather hazy. One account stated that a divorce was granted in France, where Nirdlinger was a frequent visitor, but that is not clear. In 1922, Franz Voelker, secretary of the Atlantic City Board of Taxation, sued Nirdlinger for $150,000 for "alienation of the affections of his wife." The jury awarded Voelker six cents in damages.

Unsurprisingly, Fred and Charlotte's marriage was rather rocky. The couple maintained a home at 25 South Laclede Place in Atlantic City but were often in Paris or Nice, France. Fred apparently not only had a wandering eye but was also insanely jealous with a tendency toward violence. Although neither fault was specified publicly, Charlotte successfully sued for divorce from the theater baron in 1926 but remarried him in 1928. Over the course of their two marriages, the couple had two children, Fred Jr. and Charlotte.

Charlotte Isabel Nash, Miss Saint Louis, was a contestant in the 1923 Atlantic City Beauty Pageant (the future Miss America Pageant). One of the judges, Fred Nixon-Nirdlinger, became smitten with eighteen-year-old Nash.

In March 1931, the Nirdlingers were in their apartment in Nice when Fred charged that Charlotte's attempts to learn the Italian language and her perusal of an Italian newspaper proved she had an Italian lover, which she vigorously denied. He put his hands around her throat and began to choke her, and she pulled out a revolver she had stowed under a pillow and shot him twice, killing him. Charlotte called the police immediately afterward, and they took her into custody, noting that there were visible red marks on her throat. She was charged with manslaughter.

The trial, held in May, was a circus. The French police had to keep the crowds of the curious away from the courtroom, and "Riviera playboys and girls" established a betting line on the outcome. The odds in favor of acquittal were twenty to one. Charlotte appeared on the witness stand dressed in mourning for the husband she had shot. Although the judge sharply questioned her about an alleged affair with a swimming instructor, which she emphatically denied, the prosecution was far from vigorous, with one correspondent reporting that it sounded more like a defense. The Nirdlinger children's nursemaid testified that Charlotte was "never out alone" and that her husband read every letter she sent or received. Fred's friend and attorney Charles Loeb testified that Fred had suffered severely from "the disease of jealousy."

In summing up, Charlotte's defense attorney declared that "she is too beautiful to be bad." The jury agreed and acquitted her in fifteen minutes. Charlotte returned to the United States and sold her Atlantic City home two years later. It still stands and was up for sale recently. No one seems to have missed Fred.

A New Jersey publicity program less likely to turn out like Charlotte's was the baby parade, also designed to draw tourists to the New Jersey shore. Baby parades were a very big thing up and down the Jersey coast in the 1920s and 1930s, highlighting the summer season. The most famous one was held in Asbury Park, but other towns, including Wildwood and Cape May, participated in the craze, with one report noting that "bright

Above: Mrs. Nirdlinger and her family on their return to Atlantic City from France after she disposed of Mr. Nirdlinger.

Opposite, top: The Nirdlinger home in Atlantic City. As of this writing, it still stands.

Opposite, bottom: Asbury Park baby parade in 1925.

Above: Wildwood baby parade, 1932.

Opposite, left: Gilda Gray doing her "shimmy."

Opposite, right: Baby parade Gilda Gray impersonator.

costumes and striking floats marked the carnival" held in Wildwood on August 19, 1932.

Baby parade participants were dressed by their parents to represent cultural and historic iconic figures, particularly from New Jersey but also national and international. One unusual impersonation was that of Mary Smith of Philadelphia, who participated in the 1928 Wildwood Parade as "Gilda Gray." Although she is long forgotten today, everyone knew who Gilda Gray was in 1928, when little Mary imitated her "shimmy" down the Wildwood boardwalk.

The real Gilda Gray was born Maryanna Michalska in Krakow, Poland, then part of the Austro-Hungarian empire, in 1901 and came to the United States as a child with her parents in 1909. The family settled in Milwaukee, Wisconsin. Maryanna married early, reportedly at the age of fourteen, although one account says she was twelve. She had a son the following year.

In a classic rags-to-riches story, Maryanna became a dancer in Chicago, was spotted by an agent whose wife was Sophie Tucker and ended up in New York, where she changed her name to Gilda Gray and "gave the first great impetus to the postwar era of wiggle and swiggle in night life" in 1919, with her "shimmy" dance. She performed in vaudeville and on Broadway and also starred in a number of films in the 1920s.

Gilda went through several husbands and a bankruptcy in the stock market crash of 1929 and won awards from the Polish government in exile during World War II for her support of refugees. Her finances went up and down over the years, and the Motion Picture Relief Fund paid for her funeral after her death from a heart attack on December 22, 1959. Mary Smith's life was likely much more mundane.

Baby parades were considered significant enough to draw New Jersey governors, mayors and other politicians to attend and bestow awards. Congressman and future governor Harold Hoffman attended many parades and entered his daughters as participants. New Jersey governor A. Harry Moore and Asbury Park mayor Clarence Hetrick greeted "Queen Titania" at the Asbury Park Baby Parade in 1929.

The Ohio-born Hetrick moved with his family in 1887 to Neptune, where he became the first Monmouth County student to win an academic scholarship to Rutgers University, graduating in 1895. Politically active early on, Hetrick gained a reputation as a budget whiz while tax collector of Neptune Township and, in 1906, treasurer of Asbury Park. He was elected as Monmouth County sheriff in 1907, despite rumors that, although

Asbury Park baby parade, with Mayor Hettrick awarding the winner.

married into an old county family, he had a mistress who worked at the Keystone Laundry.

In 1911, Sheriff Hetrick prevented the lynching and proved the innocence of an African American man falsely accused of a murder charge, gaining the gratitude of Asbury Park's African American community—and their votes. He was elected mayor in 1915. A Progressive Republican who was a Teddy Roosevelt Bull Moose Party supporter, Hetrick was in sync with the changing cultural and political world of the Jazz Age. His time as mayor extended into the 1920s, and he built a new high school, appointed the first woman as city clerk, promoted women's suffrage and hired African Americans, Italians, Catholics and Jews as city employees for the first time.

Hetrick was a "wet Republican" who opposed Prohibition and incurred the ire of the Anti-Saloon League and, in the 1920s, the revived Ku Klux Klan. In the mid-1920s, the Klan, allied with a Methodist minister, charged Hetrick and his associates with holding an orgy at a nearby Ocean Township speakeasy. The charges were dismissed by a grand jury, and Hetrick ran for reelection in 1927 with a public anti-Klan stance and won overwhelmingly.

The popular mayor developed a dark side, though, as a Jersey Shore political boss akin to Atlantic City's Enoch "Nucky" Johnson, whom he viewed as a rival. Mysterious boardwalk fires led to no-bid contracts for Asbury Park replacement buildings intended to rival Atlantic City, and the mayor became a rich man without any apparent outside employment. He was then hired as a "confidential advisor" to a wealthy executive, became a lobbyist with apartments in New York and Washington and was connected to several sleazy deals. Hetrick lost the election of 1933 but was returned to office and remained mayor until his death in 1941.

A more exciting 1920s public spectator sport than mayor watching was barnstorming aircraft stunts, which swept the United States entertainment scene. Pilots in surplus World War I airplanes toured the country with them and/or their passengers performing sensational tricks for enthusiastic audiences. One significant wing walker was Newark, New Jersey native Philip "Jersey" Ringel. Born in 1895, Ringel was a pilot instructor during World War I and embarked on a daredevil career after the war, doing stunts for the public and also doubling for actors in film scenes. Ringel died in an airplane crash in 1930—ironically, not while attempting aerial stunts.

Another aerial amateur stunt man was Eddie Graf, who worked at his brother's garage on Main Street in Hanover, New Jersey, but had a good sideline gig. On Sundays, he would drive to a local airfield and "provide thrills for the crowd" by "jumping from a plane with a parachute." Eddie's

Above: Jersey Ringel stunting on a plane wing.

Opposite: Eddie Graf, parachute entertainer, got stuck on this utility pole.

pilot was an experienced aviator who had served in the British Air Service in World War I.

On Sunday, November 24, 1929, after Eddie leaped from the aircraft at 1,200 feet, his parachute opened and "his descent began in earnest." When he was halfway down, however, Graf "struck an air current and the wind carried him away from the field," dumping him on some telephone wires thirty-five feet above the ground.

A crowd gathered below the wires and stared at the dangling parachutist. Although someone had a camera, no one had a ladder. Graf tried to walk across the wires but quickly abandoned that idea. Finally, a man shinnied up a pole and tossed him a rope, which he used to reach the pole and, ultimately, the ground.

Asked by a reporter if he would resume his part-time job the following Sunday, Graf responded, "Sure, why not," adding that he had ended up in trees five times after a jump but that this was his first experience dangling from phone wires. Graf went on to explain to the journalist that "some

people have the idea that we just float down but it's more like jumping out a second story window. Landing is the hard part." The reporter added that "when Graf lands he lands right, except, of course, when he lands in trees—or in telephone wires."

Some folks who craved attention from the masses went up in the air and stayed there for a while. Flagpole sitting became a popular sport to watch for many in the 1920s. In 1929, Alvin "Shipwreck" Kelly settled in atop a fifty-nine-foot flagpole on the roof of the Hotel Saint Francis in Newark, New Jersey, for a twelve-day stay. Shipwreck—who had served in the navy in World War I and would serve in the Merchant Marine in World War II and had a career as a vaudevillian and flagpole sitter in between—touted his accomplishments, although a newspaper noted that "sporting experts, however, predicted flagpole sitting contests would not gain popularity." The practice pretty much died during the Depression and, although it resurfaced on occasion in the 1940s and 1950s, never regained its 1920s popularity.

One unique and little-known aspect of 1920s culture oddly reflected future events. Moses Littaner, a "hippie" long before his time, appeared in New Jersey. In the summer of 1921, Littaner, a long-haired, bearded guy who had "fled New York," rolled into Plainfield, New Jersey, a seemingly unlikely location to establish what he called a "naturist colony." He looked at the hills beyond the town, however, and decided he was in the right place.[55]

A reporter interviewed Littaner in July, by which time he had established his "colony" of sixty people in the Watchung Mountains beyond Plainfield. The journalist "found Moses Littaner naturalistically clothed in a heavy suit of tan, a biblical beard, long flowing locks and BVDs." The proto-hippie leader called his movement "Naturism" and said it was based on "two tenets," those being "humanitarianism and vegetarianism."

Although described as vegetarians, the members of the colony were, in modern terms, vegans. Littaner told the reporter that "dairy food comes from animal life—I wouldn't touch it." He claimed that his people lived on "a dollar a week" eating raw oats, cornmeal and vegetables from their garden. There was a little magic at play as well, apparently, as Littaner claimed his "long hair attracts magnetic forces from nature" and declared his Messianic purpose in life to "lead and help others to lead a natural life." Shortly afterward, he and his entourage disappeared, no doubt in a time travel machine to reappear in California in 1969.[56]

Perhaps the most significant New Jersey public artwork of the decade was the "All Wars" monument erected in Newark's Military Park. Designed

Left: Shipwreck Kelly atop a flagpole.

Right: Amateur New Jersey flagpole sitter.

by famed sculptor Gutzon Borglum and cast in five bronze sections in Italy, the massive project, begun in 1921, was completed in 1926 and unveiled on Memorial Day. It was a tribute to the soldiers of American conflicts from the Revolution to World War I and contains "forty-two humans and two horses." Borglum was also the creator of the 1911 "seated Lincoln" in front of the Essex County Courthouse, another classic example of his work. Both were financed by Newark businessman Amos Van Horn. The Lincoln statue, dedicated by Theodore Roosevelt, has long been a favorite of Newark's youth, many of whom have had their photo taken sitting on the bench next to the president.[57]

There were a number of other statues erected to honor the military in New Jersey in the 1920s, including the Princeton monument commemorating the critical Revolutionary War battle, designed by well-known sculptor Frederick MacMonnies and dedicated by President Harding in 1922. There were other monuments by less notable sculptors erected around the state during the 1920s, most of them dedicated to local World War I veterans. Unique

Opposite, top: Moses Littaner, a "hippie" long before his time.

Opposite, bottom: Littaner's cult members harvesting vegetables.

Above: Sculptor Gutzon Borglum inspects his project, the *Wars of America* statues in Newark's Military Park.

Right: Borglum's seated Lincoln in front of the Essex County Courthouse, one of Newark's most popular monuments.

President Warren Harding dedicates Princeton monument, May 1922. Governor Edwards is seated.

ones included the Newark monument, which featured statues of ancient naked Greek soldiers instead of Americans, and the statue of a Red Cross woman ambulance driver installed at the New Jersey College for Women in New Brunswick in 1928, which disappeared over the following years—some say sacrificed to a World War II scrap drive.

Although most Americans remained skeptical regarding the purpose and outcome of World War I, they followed in the tradition established by Civil War veterans, who had erected monuments to their comrades all over the state and on battlefields. As with the Civil War memorial movement in the late nineteenth century, many of these statues of soldiers mounted atop pedestals were produced by factories. The most notable local World War I memorial was created by sculptor Charles Keck in 1924 and still stands in Montclair.

Statue of a female World War I ambulance driver at the New Jersey College for Women.

It is generally recognized by film history fans, although little known to many in the general public, that the movie industry had its origins in New Jersey. Thomas Edison opened what was the first film studio in the world at his West Orange, New Jersey laboratories to produce his Kinetoscope films. On January 4, 1894, an experimental film of Thomas Edison's employee Fred Ott sneezing was produced in the studio dubbed the "Black Maria" by Edison's workers. It was the first motion picture copyrighted in the United States. Ott, a longtime Edison worker, was the inventor's favorite employee.

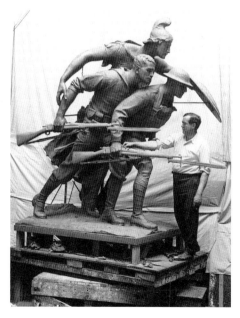

Montclair World War I Memorial, 1924, by sculptor Charles Keck.

Burlington, New Jersey World War I monument, with a National Guardsman, a Red Cross lady and a Civil War veteran. It was dedicated in 1924.

The Black Maria gained its nickname from the film crews who worked there and compared its dark and stuffy confines to the interior of a police wagon of the same nickname. Edison called it the doghouse, but that name didn't stick. The studio building was essentially a tarpaper shack with a retractable roof and rotating turntable to allow maximum light in during daylight hours. It was used for a number of Edison's pioneering short films of popular attractions of the day, including vaudeville performers, boxers and even cockfights. Annie Oakley, a resident of nearby Nutley, filmed shooting tricks in the Black Maria with a .22-caliber rifle, the

Edison's "Black Maria" film set building.

bullets passing through the tarpaper and out into the West Orange countryside.

In 1900, Edison built a rooftop movie studio in New York City. He closed the Black Maria in January 1901 and tore it down in 1903. A reproduction of the West Orange studio was constructed in May 1940 to promote the film *Edison the Man*, which featured Spencer Tracy as the legendary inventor and had multiple premieres in theaters in West Orange, East Orange, South Orange and Orange. The current version of the studio at the National Historic Park in West Orange was built by the National Park Service in 1954.

Making films in enclosed studios required access to natural light from skylights and other sources. This attribute was lacking in New York City, but across the Hudson River, there was a lot of natural light and space to build stages and other buildings necessary to filmmaking. The interior scenes in the 1903 classic *The Great Train Robbery* were filmed at Edison's New York City stage, and all exterior shots were filmed in sections of Essex County, New Jersey.

By 1915, New Jersey was the epicenter of filmmaking. Stars of the era plied their craft in the state, including Mary Pickford, Lionel Barrymore and Theda Bara, but by a mere five years later, the business had begun to shift to California, with its good year-round climate and natural light. And so, the Jersey boom went bust. Hollywood dates its birth as the nation's leading motion picture production site to 1923.

Small independent filmmakers took up the craft in New York and New Jersey in the 1920s, including African American filmmaker Oscar Micheaux, who shot his 1920 film *Symbol of the Unconquered* in Fort Lee. Micheaux's work accurately depicts the Ku Klux Klan as a terrorist organization, a rejoinder to D.W. Griffiths's 1915 racist *The Birth of a Nation*, which portrayed the Klan as saviors of southern white people. By the end of the decade, as sound began to come to films, local New Jersey small producers started making films in Yiddish and Italian for overseas markets.[58]

Another popular entertainment of the era was the public's obsession with murder trials, and one of the biggest occurred in New Jersey at the beginning of the decade. On September 22, 1922, Reverend Edward Wheeler Hall, an Episcopal priest in New Brunswick, was found shot dead along with his mistress, Eleanor Reinhardt Mills, a member of the church choir, in De Russey's Lane in Franklin Township. Suspicion fell on Reverend Hall's wife, Frances, and her brothers, but there were no indictments. The crime became popularly known as the Hall-Mills murders.

Continued newspaper speculation on the Hall-Mills murders led Governor A. Harry Moore to request a new inquiry into the case in 1926. The investigation led to indictments of Reverend Hall's widow, Frances Hall, and her brothers for murder and a trial that began on November 3 and lasted thirty days. Although the accused had the motive and ability to commit the murders, the evidence to convict them—especially the erratic testimony of the "pig woman," Jane Gibson, a farmer on whose property the bodies were found and whose claim to be a witness provided a prime rationale for the indictments—was not convincing to the jury, and they were acquitted. The case was national news and drew famous reporters from across the country. It was the biggest New Jersey crime story of the day. A recent book claims that it inspired a similar murder scene in F. Scott Fitzgerald's novel *The Great Gatsby*.

Another case to make the national news was the murder of A. William Lilliendahl in South Vineland. His wife, Margaret, and her lover, Willis Beach, were accused of the crime. The ensuing trial resulted in the invasion of May's Landing by the "H.M.T.L. (Husband Murder Trial Legion)" of reporters and photographers, eager to provide entertainment, much of it unrelated to the murder itself, for people across the country. Noted fiction

Opposite, top: Where the bodies of the minister and choir lady were found, initiating the Hall-Mills case.

Opposite, bottom: Reverend Hall's wife and family at the murder trial.

Left: Margaret Lilliendahl at her trial.

Opposite, left: Harry Thaw (*left*) at an Atlantic City beach.

Opposite, right: Evelyn Nesbit.

writer and celebrity journalist Damon Runyan, who covered the trial for the Hearst newspapers, observed that Margaret was a "a passionate type of woman" and described Beach as "the hottest man in his home township, even if he is not as young as he used to be." Runyon sat behind Margaret during the trial and observed that "Mrs. Lilliendahl uses a brand of perfume known as *Incarnat*, made by Piver. I offer this information for the benefit of my lady readers."

Another reporter was puzzled as to why the "tall and stately Mrs. Lilliendahl" was attracted to the "short and dumpy" Beach, who local people oddly regarded as an "ardent Lothario" and the "Don Juan of the countryside." Yet another writer noted that Margaret's "dominant characteristic" was her "buck teeth." Margaret's demeanor was compared unfavorably with that of Frances Hall, who, also accused of her husband's murder, had taken the stand at the recent Hall-Mills trial. The accused were found guilty and sentenced to prison.

Scoundrels who gained national attention often ended up in New Jersey, and following their exploits became another popular form of entertainment. One such was Harry Kendall Thaw, born into a wealthy family in Pittsburgh. Like almost every other hardworking con man of the late nineteenth and early twentieth centuries, he ended up spending a lot

of time in his later years in Enoch "Nucky" Johnson's Atlantic City. There were brothels, booze, illegal gambling and the beach in the city by the sea. What more could a rich ne'er-do-well want? Early on, Thaw had attacked family servants, often while babbling "baby talk," even into adolescence. As he grew older, he lavishly expended family money on drugs, "loose women" and assorted other vices, and the family spent lavishly on attorneys and bribes to cover up his excesses.

After marrying New York showgirl Evelyn Nesbit, he traveled to Manhattan and shot and killed architect Sanford White, who he believed was a rival for Evelyn's affections and had hired men to kill him. The story of White's murder and its aftermath has been told a number of times, most notably in the film *The Girl in the Red Velvet Swing*, as well as the novel and film *Ragtime*.

Thaw, unsurprisingly, was represented by the best legal talent available at his January 1907 murder trial, which ended with a deadlocked jury. In a second trial, the jury found him insane, and he was sentenced to the Matteawan asylum for life. He was out in 1916, however, and then charged with the kidnapping, whipping and sexual assault of nineteen-year-old Frederick Gump of Kansas City. Arrested, Thaw was confined again in an asylum in Philadelphia but released as cured in 1924.

In later life, Thaw seems to have calmed down a bit but remained a shyster, refusing to pay writers he had hired in an abortive film production business. He was a popular guy in Atlantic City in the 1920s, however, where he was a frequent visitor. The Atlantic City lifeguards allegedly found Thaw to be "a great favorite, as many times he aids them in the launching of their boats and in the rescue of a drowning bather." Evelyn performed in Atlantic City while Harry was in town in 1926, and the two met for a friendly lunch. Harry K. Thaw died in Miami, Florida, in 1947 and was buried in Pittsburgh.

It is difficult to find a chapter slot to fit another bizarre character of the era, Dr. Henry Andrews Cotton, a psychiatrist born in 1876 in Norfolk, Virginia, who was medical director of the Trenton, New Jersey State Mental Hospital between 1907 and 1930. His medical ideas were absurd by modern standards, to say the least, but his portrayal in the HBO series *Boardwalk Empire* lets us slip him into the cultural realm, as a representative of medical concepts unique to his era.

Dr. Cotton was an enthusiastic proponent of the "surgical bacteriology" theory, which posited that mental disorders were the result of bacterial or virological infections in the body and that there was, therefore, a surgical cure for them. In 1921, he wrote a book on his theories titled *The Defective Delinquent and Insane: The Relation of Focal Infections to Their Causation, Treatment and Prevention.*

Cotton claimed the Trenton hospital he ran was "no longer an asylum nor custodial institution but is to be looked upon as a curative institution or hospital in every sense of the word" in a speech to a convention of New Jersey physicians in Spring Lake. His subject was the treatment of paresis and locomotor ataxia (a condition of paralysis and dementia in the later stages of syphilis) and curing those ailments through speedy treatment. He maintained that such treatment, which he did not elaborate on, was highly effective, resulting in a 35.5 percent complete cure and a 22 percent improvement rate.

Cotton began patient treatment by extracting teeth and then, if that did not cure the patient's mental illness, moving on to tonsils and other organs, including testicles and ovaries. In the pre-antibiotic era, such surgery could have drastic results, and Cotton admitted to a 30 percent death rate in his patients, although a later analysis proved it was closer to 45 percent. Ironically, he was in other ways a progressive, as he abolished mandatory restraints for patients and had regular staff meetings to discuss issues.

Right: Dr. Henry A. Cotton.

Below: The pipe-smoking dog at the Hoboken docks.

Perhaps surprisingly, Cotton got a lot of support, and the *New York Times* endorsed him, declaring in 1922 that his New Jersey hospital was "the most progressive institution in the world for the care of the insane" due to his "brilliant leadership."

Despite all the praise, Cotton's theories became controversial in some medical circles. Dr. Phyllis Greenacre, assigned to investigate his work, described Cotton as a "singularly peculiar" individual and noted that when she tried to interview patients at his hospital, they were often unintelligible because all their teeth had been removed. The criticism of Greenacre and some other doctors led to a New Jersey state senate hearing on Cotton in 1925. He became ill with a "nervous breakdown" during the hearing and self-diagnosed his problem as caused by infected teeth. He had several pulled and declared himself cured.

Henry Andrews Cotton retired as medical director of the hospital in 1930 and died of a heart attack in 1933, but not before opining to the press as "an internationally known alienist" that Giuseppe Zangara, who had tried to assassinate President-elect Franklin D. Roosevelt, was incited to do so due to "stomach pains," apparently a not uncommon ailment for mentally deranged presidential assassins. Cotton was posthumously lauded by journalists in his obituaries as a pioneering figure in American mental health treatment.

If you were looking for less serious forms of entertainment than husband killers or unbalanced doctors, you could go to Hoboken, where an old man sat down at the train station with his dog that would smoke a pipe on command in exchange for a small donation.

Chapter 4

TRANSPORTATION

I t was a spectacular event that drew thousands of eager participants from every section of the state, a day that included a parade, rousing vaudeville entertainment provided by a troupe of acrobats and a brilliant fireworks display. The opening of the Victory Bridge, an eight-thousand-foot-long span across the Raritan River connecting Perth Amboy and Sayreville, New Jersey, was a monumental achievement that reflected the state's enormous strides to meet the increasing needs of the automobile age. The bridge's grand opening, held on June 25, 1926, was yet another milestone on the road to accommodating the ever-increasing number of motorists traversing the Garden State.

The Victory Bridge, equipped with a turning span to accommodate ships, was the longest such structure of its time, spanning 360 feet. It replaced an inferior "county bridge" that was unable to handle the traffic volume and weight of increasingly larger trucks.

Former governor George S. Silzer, who, as we have noted, was a supporter of transportation projects, was one of the many dignitaries to speak at the grand opening. He described the bridge as "a victory of peace" and "good government" because it was "erected by the government for the common people who couldn't do something for themselves." The structure, he added, was "built honestly and there hasn't been a hint or suggestion of graft." The fact that he said that is somewhat revelatory in itself.

The daylong grand opening drew more than sixty thousand celebrants and included a concert and dancing on the bridge. Perth Amboy was filled

The alleged first car in Trenton.

The Victory Bridge.

with "hawkers" selling hot dogs, soda water and ice cream. In addition, "the balloon vendors were making a rich harvest while the flower girls went home with their purses well-filled." The jubilant crowd ended the day watching fireworks from the span.[59]

Unfortunately, the euphoria over the architectural achievement was short-lived. Anticipated traffic was grossly underestimated. Within a few years, the bridge was crammed with frazzled drivers and overheated cars, particularly during the summer months when North Jersey residents flocked to the Shore. In addition, the increase in pleasure boating led to frequent openings of the span, exacerbating the traffic jams.

By the summer of 1929, state highway commissioner Abraham Jelin was lamenting that "a terrible situation has arisen…and steps for relief should be initiated." The commission ordered an immediate study of traffic congestion at the bridge. Eventually, the beleaguered structure would be supported by a second span, the Edison Bridge, linking Woodbridge and Sayreville, which opened in 1940.

The failure of the Victory Bridge to alleviate overwhelming traffic congestion was representative of the challenges faced by 1920s planners and legislators. Despite herculean efforts to create a serviceable road system, the relentlessly increasing onslaught of motorists could not be appeased.

By 1924, transportation officials were stressing the importance of constructing a comprehensive road system to accommodate traffic volume. Highway commissioner Jelin noted that the lack of adequate roads was disrupting the state's all-important tourism industry. Discussing Shore route traffic, Jelin testified at a meeting of the American Road Builders Association that "congestion is so great now that people are actually keeping their automobiles in the garages on Sunday rather than to ride in the traffic existing." Jelin posited, "Any wonder that we feel that the road problems in New Jersey are perhaps greater than in any other state in the union?"[60]

On a national level, the need for better roads was apparent well before World War I and became even more evident during the war years, when heavy trucks moving supplies across the country punished the nation's road system. The abysmal state of the country's roadways became apparent when it took a convoy of U.S. Army vehicles sixty-two days to travel from coast to coast.

Across the country, motorists clamored for more and better hard-surfaced, all-weather roads and for shifting some of the fiscal responsibility to higher levels of government. A breakthrough was accomplished with the Federal Aid Act in 1916, which provided $75 million in aid for states with highway departments. At the urging of then governor Walter E. Edge, the New Jersey legislature created a state Highway Department in 1917, governed by a state Highway Commission. At the same time, the legislature created a basic highway system, designating fifteen routes as the primary concern of the new department.

Perhaps the most iconic of the state's roads of the era was the section of the Lincoln Highway, a transcontinental route named after President Abraham Lincoln, that started in Times Square and wended its way through New Jersey as part of its countrywide journey. The road, the brainchild of entrepreneur Carl Fisher, was intended to be a significant step forward in replacing the rutted dirt roads that then crisscrossed the state and country.

New Jersey governor Walter Edge.

The first section of the highway to be completed ran from Newark to Jersey City and was dedicated in 1913. As more sections were completed, the route headed southwest into the heart of New Jersey, following the path of today's Route 27, passing through towns that included Rahway, Edison and Trenton.

By 1920, its supporters marveled at the influx of tourists—and money—that the road generated. "Each year sees the volume of tourist traffic upon the Highway increasing," proclaimed an editorial in the *Central Jersey Home News*. "This means new people in each community; new money in each community; new money in circulation in amounts literally running into millions of dollars."[61]

Joining the Lincoln Highway were myriad other roadways and massive improvements during the 1920s that laid the groundwork for the intricate road system of today. It was a bustling time of nonstop construction and innovation, including the introduction of three-lane highways, divided highways and, to combat the headache of congested intersections, the traffic circle, the first of which was the Airport Circle in Pennsauken, New Jersey, which served a route from Philadelphia to the Jersey Shore. Nightclubs and other attractions such as the Whoopee Coaster, an automotive-themed roller coaster, sprang up around the circle, making it a destination in itself.

One of the most spectacular and awe-inspiring developments of the era was the construction of massive bridges and tunnels that forever altered the

New Jersey landscape and opened up vast new travel opportunities for New Jersey and neighboring states' motorists.

An imposing example of these structures was the Pulaski Skyway, a four-lane bridge-causeway that vaulted over the Hackensack and Passaic Rivers and the Jersey meadows, cutting travel time from Jersey City to Newark from twenty-five to five minutes. It was begun in the 1920s, and when completed, despite political and labor conflicts between unions and political boss Frank Hague, the elevated bridge and highway enabled frazzled drivers to avoid two busy drawbridges and numerous traffic lights. It also contributed to the early success of Newark Airport; in conjunction with the Holland Tunnel, it allowed air passengers landing at Newark to arrive in New York City in a matter of minutes. There have been problems with the Skyway, named for Polish general Casimir Pulaski, who trained and led American troops during the Revolution. Perhaps the most visible issue is that entryways to the road are on the left, not the usual right, and there are no road shoulders. This feature was due to the fact that the bridge designer's previous work was with railroad routes.

The Holland Tunnel was another major catalyst for improved transportation in northern New Jersey. The Hudson River had long stood as a barrier between the state and Manhattan, which made the area dependent on ferryboats. Urban planners originally considered a motor vehicle bridge to span the waterway. Prohibitive costs, however, convinced officials to consider a tunnel instead. In 1919, construction of a vehicular tunnel was authorized under the supervision of Clifford M. Holland, whose experience in building the subway tunnels under the East River made him the logical candidate for the post of chief engineer.

Holland's plan called for two cast-iron tubes lined with concrete, each providing a roadbed for two lanes of vehicular traffic and an elevated pedestrian walk. The undertaking was a dangerous one. As workers at each end of the tunnel inched their way through the silt and sand of the riverbed, the pressure of seventy feet of water above them constantly threatened to burst into the working chamber. The Hudson River was held back by generating an equal amount of pressure within the chamber using compressed air, sometimes at a force of over forty-five pounds per square inch above normal. This enormous pressure and the associated heat created grueling conditions for the unfortunate workers. Known as "sandhogs," the tunnel laborers could remain in the tunnel only for a designated period and had to undergo controlled decompression when exiting the structure. Otherwise, workers risked suffering from generalized barotrauma, popularly

Left: Pulaski Skyway under construction.

Below: Pulaski Skyway.

Opposite: Holland Tunnel under construction.

known as "the bends," with symptoms that included joint pain, headaches and visual disturbances.

The tunnel, initially called the Hudson River Vehicular Tunnel or the Canal Street Tunnel, was renamed the Holland Tunnel after Chief Engineer Holland, who died in 1924 of a heart attack, brought on, according to some, as a result of his "nervous breakdown" due to the stress of tunnel construction. It was dedicated and opened to traffic in November 1927. Governor A. Harry Moore waxed optimistic about the tunnel's significance: "From this day on there will stream ceaselessly through its length lines of pleasure and commercial traffic in two directions, creating a better understanding of each happier acquaintance."[62]

James Gormley of Passaic, one of the first motorists to enter the tunnel after its official midnight opening, joined a lineup of several hundred cars gathered at the entrance, "all eager to experience the novelty of crossing to New York City under water." Gormley made the trip to New York in seven minutes and immediately returned to New Jersey, making that trip in six minutes. The Holland Tunnel was named a National Historic Civil and Mechanical Engineering Landmark in 1982 and a National Historic Landmark in 1993.[63]

Above: The first cars through the Holland Tunnel come out in New York.

Opposite: Ben Franklin Bridge across the Delaware.

While work was moving forward on the Holland Tunnel, another major initiative was underway in South Jersey, as planners grappled with a way to cross the lower Delaware River. Their solution was the massive Benjamin Franklin Bridge, or Delaware River Bridge, as it was initially called, which linked Camden and Philadelphia. The structure, the longest suspension bridge in the world at the time of its completion in 1926, was just under 3,200 feet long. The $37 million span featured six lanes for vehicular traffic, with additional space reserved for trolley tracks.

The remarkable surge of road, bridge and tunnel construction in the 1920s reflected the public's insatiable appetite for auto travel. Each year, traffic volume increased at a remarkable rate, as New Jerseyans' preoccupation with the automobile only intensified. A 1927 ad for Marchese Auto Sale Co. in Passaic captured the car-buying fever of the era. "Drive a Car and Begin to Live" trumpeted the ad, which boasted of deals such as a Studebaker Sedan for $387. "Your family—your Father and Mother—your Wife—or the Girl

Friend will also enjoy the thrill of motoring," the ad proclaimed. "You can add many hours of happiness to your own and the lives of your friends and family with a car." Unlike scheduled public transportation, automobiles gave owners the ability to go wherever they wanted whenever they wanted, providing that the roads were drivable.[64]

When buying a car, one article noted, it was the woman who chose the vehicle. "Men buy automobiles—but it is the woman who chooses them," the story noted. One of the most appealing automobile features for a woman, according to a store manager quoted in the piece, was "good lines." The manager added, "She can appreciate symmetry of design and she knows when anything has that peculiar quality we call balance." Condescendingly relegated to the role of passenger, women were depicted as visualizing themselves riding regally in the vehicle: "She thinks how the car will set off the gown to advantage. And the picture pleases her."[65]

In daily life, however, women were frequently behind the wheel and often faced criticism from their male counterparts, who contended they were inferior drivers. In 1926, disgruntled female members of the New Jersey Automobile and Motor Club besieged the clubhouse "following a traffic officer's complaint that nine out of ten violations of traffic rules were women," according to a news story in the *Ridgewood Herald*. "They were especially wrought over the quotations from him in a newspaper story, that 99 percent of women can't drive a car and that they 'won't put their minds on the car, the rules and the traffic,'" the article noted.[66]

An auto show at the Roseville Avenue Armory in Newark.

Some New Jersey women were more adventurous than the average male driver. Alice Huyler Ramsey set a precedent for the state's daring and skilled women. Born Alice Huyler in Hackensack, she had a natural mechanical talent, which was encouraged by her father. Huyler took shop courses at Hackensack High School, graduating in 1903. She left Vassar College to marry John Rathbone Ramsey, who encouraged her nontraditional interests and adventurous spirit, which led her, in 1909, to become the first woman to drive across the United States. She continued driving into her nineties and was named "Woman Motorist of the Twentieth Century" by the American Automobile Association in 1960.

Ridgewood police chief James A. McRell refuted the assertions of female lack of skill in motoring, noting that although women may not be the best drivers, they were the most careful. According to McRell, "Women have fewer accidents by far than men; nowhere near as many women are warned by our traffic men, and a whole lot less {not over 10 percent} actually violate the regulations."[67]

A 1922 incident involving Bayonne High School senior Henrietta Stabile, voted "most popular woman driver" in Hudson County but who accidentally drove her car into a jitney bus, "shaking up" several of the passengers, seemed to contradict the chief's conclusions. But both sexes

Alice Huyler changing a tire on her cross-country drive.

were often guilty of sloppy driving and poor motoring etiquette, as noted in a 1926 story in the *Monmouth Inquirer*. David Van Schaack, vice president of the National Safety Council, advised motorists to avoid driver don'ts such as cavalierly honking the horn. "Don't signal thusly to attract the attention of people inside houses," Schaack noted. "Remember, some folks sleep at all hours of the day, some are sick or nervous and your honking will annoy them."[68]

Schaack also cautioned against flirting while motoring. "Don't think that because you are in an automobile you are privileged to attempt to vamp every pretty girl who passes your machine," he advised. Perhaps most importantly, drivers were urged to keep their poise if they were involved in an accident. "Swearing at the other party is not only decidedly poor etiquette but bad judgment," Schaack observed. "Both of you may get hurt or end up in a police cell."[69]

The combination of heavy traffic and careless driving led to accidents, and children were particularly at risk of injury. Police captain Charles Humes of Camden told a reporter in 1929 that officials were especially concerned about the safety of young pedestrians, particularly since Camden was considered one of the most dangerous cities in the country in terms of traffic accidents and fatalities. Humes called for a concerted effort on the part of parents and teachers to educate children to use greater care in crossing streets.

"The number of accidents resulting from children dashing helter-skelter across the streets increases daily and will continue to do so until the child is deeply impressed with the necessity of crossing the street only at the properly designated points," Humes said.[70]

It wasn't only children who carelessly crossed streets. Jaywalking was a normal procedure for adults who grew up in the horse and carriage days. On July 12, 1923, Newark's police officers were informed that "crossing the street in the middle of the block, walking diagonally from corner to corner or walking against a stream of traffic" was now a "crime in Newark… punishable by a fine of from $2 to $25 [$28 to $350 in today's money]." Public safety director William J. Brennan was asked to enforce the regulation "to cut down the fatalities at Broad and Market streets." Citizens were given a thirty-day grace period to get used to the new law. Some, used to crossing a street wherever they wished in the days of horse and wagon and trolley traffic, never did.

While planners and law enforcement officials grappled with the challenges of the traffic boom, other modes of travel also rose to the forefront, particularly air travel. A rapid increase in public interest in flying was due to many spectacular events, including Charles Lindbergh's nonstop flight from New York to Paris in 1927.

An airfield in Atlantic City was opened in 1910 by George Ulizio, an entrepreneur and real estate broker who saw a market for air service to what was, at the time, a significant national resort. Ulizio's field was certified to accept passenger aircraft in 1911 and was the first municipal facility in the country to handle both seaplanes and conventional aircraft. It was also allegedly, in a 1919 newspaper article, the first airfield referred to as an "airport." On July 8, 1922, Atlantic City purchased the airport and renamed it Bader Field, after Atlantic City mayor Edward Bader, a protégé of famed Atlantic City political boss Enoch "Nucky" Johnson.

In the early 1920s, people in southern New Jersey felt there was a dire need for a new airport in the Greater Philadelphia area. The existing airport in Pennsylvania was in an inconvenient location to serve the city's needs, and so Camden, on the New Jersey side of the Delaware, with its new bridge spanning the river, seemed an appropriate site for a new airfield. It had to be in a semirural area because smokestacks and tall buildings hindered takeoffs and landings by the small aircraft of the era. The site chosen was on undeveloped farmland along the Cooper River near Crescent Boulevard in Pennsauken.

A police officer attempts to stop a lady jaywalker in Newark, New Jersey, in 1922.

Everybody jaywalks in 1914 Newark.

Bader Field in Atlantic City in 1920.

Crescent Airport opened in September 1929 and instantly became the prime airfield in the Philadelphia metropolitan area. Virtually all mail and passengers destined for the city across the river landed at Crescent. The adjacent area, including a traffic circle, another transportation novelty of the era, also became a magnet site, with several nightclubs, a swimming pool, a boxing arena and a dog racing track. In the 1930s, it also served as a training field for marine and naval pilots.

By World War II, however, Crescent Airport was in decline, as larger passenger and transport aircraft requiring longer runways became the norm. The opening of Philadelphia International Airport in 1940 resulted in major airlines leaving Crescent and moving to the more modern field. Although it limped along into the 1950s, Crescent was doomed. It closed in 1956 and eventually became the site of an industrial park.

In Newark, interest in a "flying field" had begun to percolate in the early 1920s, fueled by the city's commercial and transportation rivalry with New York. Lacking New York City's deep-water harbor and expansive shoreline, and although Hoboken was considered a vital part of the port of New York, Newark could not compete in seaborne transport. An airport, however, was a different matter.

In 1927, Newark officials announced the start of construction of Newark Airport, which opened in October 1928 on a one-hundred-acre tract. Though primitive by modern standards, it was one of the best equipped in the nation at the time. The airport featured paved runways, an unheard-of luxury, and twenty-two one-million-candlepower lights to aid in night landings. A single hangar, which housed twenty-five planes, was fitted with a hot air heating system to provide the constant temperature and humidity necessary to prevent warping of wooden airplane parts.

A delegate of the Passaic County freeholders who visited the site in 1928 marveled at the state-of-the-art facility and lavished praise on its supervisor, Richard Allsward. The freeholders "expressed themselves as confident that, under his able direction, the Newark airport will rapidly become one of the most attractive and important of the world's highways of air transportation," according to a news report. Freeholder William H. Young said the "prominence and importance" of the airport was best illustrated by the fact that it was visited daily by an estimated thirty thousand

Pilots and local folks check out the first of ten planes authorized for Camden's Crescent Airport in 1929.

Newark Airport under construction.

curious people. The visit ended on an exciting note with the arrival of a private plane from Miami carrying twenty passengers. "The committee was deeply interested in the arrival of the plane, which has a wing span of eighty-five feet," the news story reported. The creation of Newark Airport made it possible to create the first New Jersey National Guard air unit, the 119th Observation Squadron, which established its headquarters at the airport.[71]

Planes could be as dangerous as cars, perhaps more so. A civilian plane on a joy ride crashed into Governor Morgan Foster Larson's summer residence at the Sea Girt National Guard base, narrowly missing Larson's mother. A military plane crashed on takeoff in Shrewsbury, killing the pilot, copilot and all the occupants of the house it crashed into. Another large plane, taking a cargo of tourists from Newark Airport to fly over New York City, never made it into the air, crashing into a train at the end of the runway. All twenty passengers died. The pilot was injured but survived.

A more politically important crash occurred in the summer of 1928, when twenty-two-year-old Captain Emilio Carranza, the great-nephew of Mexican president Venustiano Carranza and a daredevil pilot known as

Newark Airport in 1929.

"Mexico's Lindbergh," or "Mex Lindy" for short, was on a goodwill tour of the United States. He flew into Lowell, Massachusetts, on June 21 to help dedicate the opening of the Lowell Airfield.

After leaving New York City on a return flight to Mexico on July 12, Carranza crashed his plane—the same model that Lindbergh flew to France—in the New Jersey Pinelands and was killed in the crash. His body was recovered the following day and brought to the garage of Willis Buzby's general store in Chatsworth, where it was placed in a makeshift coffin before being moved to Burlington and then back to Mexico.

The crash site, in Tabernacle, became a temporary tourist attraction, and local folks gathered around the wreckage of Carranza's aircraft for a photo opportunity before it was hauled away. Mexican schoolchildren contributed money for a stone pillar monument with a carved Aztec eagle plummeting toward earth that was later erected at the location, and a memorial service conducted by the Mexican consuls to New York and Philadelphia and the local American Legion post is still held there annually.

On the upside, the increased industrialization of New Jersey during World War I led to aircraft manufacturing in the state. The Standard

Opposite, top: Site of Shrewsbury crash.

Opposite, bottom: Carranza in D.C. after a flight from Mexico, 1928.

Above: Carranza monument location sign.

Right: Carranza monument.

Aircraft Corporation, founded in 1916 with headquarters in Plainfield, New Jersey, had a factory in Elizabeth and manufactured and sold light aircraft to the United States Army and Navy. In 1918, the company was licensed to build the British O/400 bomber and reportedly eventually produced more than one hundred. The Curtiss-Wright Corporation also established a number of factories across the state to manufacture airplane parts.

The revolutionary Trimotor plane intended to transport eight or nine passengers or an equivalent amount of cargo was invented by Dutch aircraft inventor Anthony Fokker, whose World War I fighter plane designs had gained fame in the German air force. The Trimotor was manufactured at Fokker's

Aircraft designer Anthony Fokker.

Atlantic Aircraft Company, founded in 1924 and located at Teterboro Airport in Hasbrouck Heights, New Jersey. Variants were later produced by the Ford Motor Company and other manufacturers.[72]

Richard Byrd led an expedition to fly over the North Pole in a Fokker Trimotor in 1926, and although his claims of success were disputed, the Fokker became the most notable aircraft of the late 1920s. Byrd's expedition was financed by Edsel Ford, son of the automobile inventor, and his plane was named for Edsel's three-year-old daughter Josephine Ford.[73]

James Cameron, a friend of author Joseph Bilby, actually took to the air as a passenger in a restored Fokker Trimotor at an airshow on Long Island in 1977 and recalled it as having "wicked seats. It was likely flying in an aluminum garden shed."[74]

While cars and planes captured the public's imagination, the railroad remained a reliable and heavily used mode of getting around New Jersey. At the end of World War I, the railroads were the principal carriers of both freight and passengers. In the movement of goods and people from city to city, more than 75 percent of freight and 80 percent of passengers traveled by rail. As the decade progressed, however, autos and buses began to erode the railroad's share of passenger traffic.

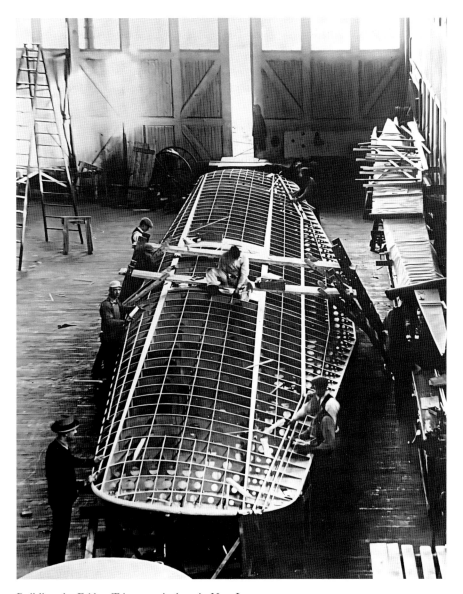

Building the Fokker Trimotor airplane in New Jersey.

C.H. Markham, who served as governmental director of railroads during World War I, observed in a 1926 *Press of Atlantic City* report that the auto and railroad industries should cooperate, not compete. "In some cases, motor vehicles are capable of furnishing better transportation than railroads, and in these instances the railroads must give way," Markham said. "On the

The Fokker plane test flight in New Jersey was named after Henry Ford's granddaughter Josephine.

other hand, there are certain transportation services that can be supplied better by railroads, and in these services the railroad must predominate."

The auto dominated in the domain of local travel, according to Markham. "The automobile, good roads and human nature are an unbeatable combination in this type of travel," he said. Although the motor car had encroached on the number of passengers taking short train trips, Markham added, it had contributed to an increase in long-distance rail travel.[75]

"Passenger automobiles and busses, on improved roads, have instilled in the public a taste for travel," the *Press* opined. "Inspired by the new vision of surrounding country given them by the motor car, people want to look beyond, like Alice in Wonderland, and see what lies past the horizon—in California, Florida, the romantic West, the historic East and the seductive Southland."[76]

Indeed, despite the public's infatuation with automobiles, railroads remained a popular mode of transportation throughout the 1920s and beyond. By the 1930s, New Jersey had more railroad track per square mile than any other state, according to a 1930s guide published by the Works Progress Administration. The system featured concentration of terminals on the west bank of the Hudson, feeders for ocean traffic, cross-river traffic to New York City and eight great trunk lines across the central and northern parts of the state. By the late 1930s, more than two thousand miles of track within the state were operated by twenty-seven railroads, of which fifteen were first class.

Ships also remained an important component of the state's transportation scene. The principal deep-water ports on the northwest border of the state were Newark and Elizabeth Port on Newark Bay, Perth Amboy on Raritan Bay and Jersey City and Bayonne on New York Bay. Hoboken, on the Hudson, long considered a major transoceanic cargo and transportation hub, became a critically important site during World War I, when the city served as the point of departure and return for soldiers from Bergen County's Camp Merritt. Following the declaration of war, the federal government seized existing German shipping company piers in Hoboken and warehouses and vessels in the city, including the Hamburg liner *Vaterland*, which had arrived in Hoboken in 1914 on its maiden voyage and was stuck there due to the start of World War I. The ship was renamed *Leviathan* and turned into a troop transport and a postwar American ocean liner.

Following the war, the Hudson County waterfront teemed with passengers arriving and departing on regular transoceanic steamship lines, which also handled freight. An April 10, 1922 news report observed that "shipping activities in Hoboken on the week-end were the busiest, it is believed, since

the war." Crowds were entranced by the sailing of the *Leviathan*, which began its journey as a major civilian ship sailing to Newport News, Virginia, for repairs and renovations.[77]

Throughout the 1920s, American newspapers featured numerous photos of politicians, entertainers and other celebrities traveling abroad, invariably by ocean liner, as regular transatlantic flight was still in the future.

A major casualty of the 1920s was the trolley, which reached a peak national ridership of fourteen billion in 1923 before slumping into a steady decline. Transit officials became aware of the cost-effectiveness of using gasoline-powered buses instead of the more expensive trolleys, which ran on electricity provided by overhead wires.

An in-depth opinion piece in the August 14, 1923 edition of Camden's *Morning Post* urged commuters to abandon the city's combined trolley and bus system in favor of buses only. The writer noted it would require three hundred "large, modern buses" to handle an estimated 120,000 passengers daily, at a cost of between $7,500 and $10,000 per bus.[78] Such an initiative would enable commuters to travel in "large, comfortable, easy riding, absolutely safe, up-to-date buses," the writer noted. "The workingman would

Opposite: Hoboken docks in the 1920s.

Above: The massive German liner *Vaterland* docking in Hoboken in 1914.

Left: Actress Kay Laurell on an ocean liner bound for Europe in 1925.

A local trolley crowded with passengers.

A Newark bus in the 1920s.

go to work in the morning, and return home in the evening, as luxuriously as his employer who uses his own limousine, and who thinks the trolley cars, in which he never rides, are good enough for his employees."[79]

The article also outlined the numerous merits of bus versus trolley travel. While buses could pull over to the side of the street to pick up passengers without causing delays, stationary trolleys held up the others behind them. "If a stranger stops a trolley car to ask questions, the two minutes' conversation may keep one thousand passengers waiting in trolley cars in line for blocks behind," the story explained.[80]

Another drawback of trolley transportation was the overhead wires used to power the vehicles, described as "the most unsightly feature of a modern city street" and "a menace to life and property." The writer asked readers to "imagine the streets of Camden free from unsightly poles and wires," adding that "if trolley wires were eliminated, it would not be long before all overhead wires were removed, and the business street would be much more attractive."[81]

When it came to the winners and losers in New Jersey's transportation scene, the automobile was clearly number one on the champions' list. The motor vehicle changed the landscape of New Jersey, accelerating the state's growth and opening up new horizons to anyone with access to a car. By the mid-1920s, planners, politicians and social observers knew the state was in the midst of a massive transformation that required an intensive effort to properly address it.

"Jersey Must Lead in Super-Highways" trumpeted a headline in the November 15, 1926 issue of the *Long Branch Daily Record*. The opinion piece asked, "With the number of automobiles in traffic doubling every three years, what are we going to do in the year 1950 for roads?" The answer was to think of "super-highways" that would accommodate the "ever-increasing use of the automobile and motor truck." The article foreshadowed the construction of the Garden State Parkway and New Jersey Turnpike, which ushered the state into a golden age of motor travel in the 1950s and '60s. The astute planning and hard labor of the 1920s laid the groundwork for a network of roads and "super-highways" of today.[82]

Boats, trains, planes and trolleys were all part of New Jersey's vibrant 1920s transportation scene, but the automobile truly defined it. The vehicle represented freedom, mobility and opportunity and continues to dominate the traveling landscape today. It all began with those first few roads, heavily traversed byways such as the Lincoln Highway, that formed the beginning network of the intricate web that connects New Jerseyans from all parts of the state.

Chapter 5

A NEW WORLD FOR THE LADIES

By 1922, the times had dramatically changed for New Jersey women, as a *Central New Jersey Home News* columnist dryly observed. "What was generally condemned yesterday is generally condoned today," the writer noted. "Take, for example, smoking by women."[83]

Indeed, smoking was only one of the many liberties that the female population enjoyed in the explosion of personal freedoms following World War I. The modern woman of the day was also inclined to "expose her shoulder and wear kneelength [*sic*] skirts with impunity," the writer complained. "If fact, she is looked upon in some circles as a bit of a frump if she doesn't."[84]

The changes had been swift and dramatic. In 1919, the typical middle-class woman wore skirts six inches above the ground, light powder—and nothing else—on her face and long hair, since short hair was considered radical and unfeminine, writes Frederick Lewis Allen in *Only Yesterday: An Informal History of the 1920s.* In a few short years, every fashionable miss wore revealing dresses, rouge and lipstick and short, boyish hair.

Physical appearance was a superficial, but nevertheless significant, manifestation of women's growing independence in 1920s New Jersey and beyond. On the labor and political fronts, the female population carved out substantial inroads, chipping away at suffocating nineteenth-century restrictions.

According to the 1920 U.S. Census, more than eight million women were gainfully employed. Of that number, more than one million were engaged

A cigar-smoking lady from Keansburg, New Kersey.

in various professional and semiprofessional pursuits, including architects, chemists, dentists and engineers. Compared to the 1910 census, the number of women employed in clerical work rose 140 percent; the number of women in public service climbed 61 percent; and women in trades rose 42 percent. This trend had its origin during World War I, when military service took many men out of the workplace.

"Women's métier is obviously the business world," declared a 1929 edition of the *Press of Atlantic City*. "Broadly speaking, those figures mean that the woman who works is increasingly demonstrating her right to the title 'business or professional' woman."[85]

The advancement of females in the workplace was celebrated during National Business Women's Week by one thousand communities across the country in March 1929. The showcase was designed as a "memorial to

the achievements of pioneer business women and as a testimonial to what women are accomplishing in the world today," according to a news article.

Alida Wheeler, a restaurant owner and operator, organized the Women's Week's activities in Atlantic City. Planned events included tributes to businesswomen by city pastors, a city library book collection dedicated to female entrepreneurs and a public relations dinner to honor working women.[86]

Opposite: Flappers on display.

Above: Female workers canning vegetables in a factory in Orange, New Jersey, in 1920.

Lurking behind the positive encouragement, however, was a broad swath of naysayers who felt women should be married and at home with their children, not laboring in an office or factory. The career woman who chose to marry "is in many cases and under ordinary conditions expected to give up her job," according to a 1923 article in the *Central New Jersey Home News*. "The consequence is that capable women who might be successful in business are often obliged to make a definite choice between marriage and a career, even though they may feel that they are as much entitled to both as a man is."[87]

Emily C. Hassmiller, executive secretary of Bayonne's City Welfare Bureau, argued that women deserved the opportunity to pursue careers, which provided a source of happiness and satisfaction. "Whether a woman chooses spinsterhood or marriage, she should have other interests as well," Hassmiller observed in a 1925 interview. "Marriage and career can both be the lot of the modern woman. People have come to the point where they no longer expect a woman to devote her entire life to her family."[88]

Those who did choose to join the male-dominated working world were encouraged to challenge the submissive stereotype perpetuated by society and practice assertiveness in the factory and office.

Lena Mades Phillips, president of the National Federation of Business and Professional Women's Clubs, urged women to advocate for themselves, particularly during salary negotiations. "Until business women learn that it is not unladylike to ask for a raise they won't get very far in the business world," Phillips declared. "Women must be sold on themselves, they must appreciate themselves and show their courage to other women. Above all they must learn their value to their employer and demand a just salary."[89]

In addition to fighting for financial parity, many advocates pushed for safe and manageable working conditions for women. For years, women's leaders pushed for legislation that would exempt females from working the overnight "graveyard" shift, 10:00 p.m. to 6:00 a.m., at factories, laundries and other establishments. Proponents of the measure argued that women felt unsafe working at night and were concerned about the welfare of their children. Other groups, such as the National Woman's Party, criticized the proposal, calling it "protective legislation" that "penalized women with children to care for during the day and put women in a special category that legitimized inequality in the workplace," according to a 1923 news report.

Despite opposition, a New Jersey no-night-work-for-women bill was signed in March 1923, during a ceremony in Trenton attended by a large delegation of women from both political parties who were instrumental in pushing the measure. Immediately after signing the bill, Governor George Silzer presented the quill pen with which he signed the measure to Mrs. G.W.B. Cushing of East Orange, president of the New Jersey Consumers' League. "This is a red-letter day in my life," she declared.[90]

In addition to greater visibility in the workplace, women gained a foothold in the political arena during the 1920s, galvanized by the Nineteenth Amendment, which recognized women's right to vote in 1920. Women had an obligation to vote, stressed New Brunswick city attorney Thomas H. Hagerty, who was the principal speaker at a Parent-Teacher Association meeting in October 1925. "Women should take a more active part in politics and not leave it to the man to exercise the right to vote," Hagerty said. "Some will say that their place is in the home but this should not draw them back from practicing the power to vote."

Hagerty praised Mary Norton, a Democrat who represented Jersey City and Bayonne in the United States House of Representatives, as an example of a woman's ability to reach great heights in the world of politics. "Mrs. Norton of Hudson County worked hard and zealously for her party," Hagerty said. "She is now the foremost lady politician in the east." Although "all ladies" were not required "to make great politicians of themselves," Hagerty added, they were urged to go out and practice their constitutional right.[91]

Mary Norton was only one of the female luminaries active in New Jersey's political scene. Thelma Parkinson was another powerful lawmaker who worked her way up the political ladder. Parkinson, a graduate of Smith College, left a career teaching English at Vineland High School to pursue a career in politics. In 1924, she was elected as a Democratic state committeewoman from Cumberland County. That same year, she acted as one of New Jersey's at-large delegates to the Democratic National Convention.

A news item at the time described Parkinson as an influential leader who "entered politics in 1921 when the political boss wanted a feminine nominee who would follow instructions." Although she "did at the start," Parkinson went on to establish her own political identity, culminating in winning the state committee position.[92] Parkinson went on to enjoy an illustrious political career. In 1930, she became the first woman to be nominated for the United States Senate in New Jersey, and although she did not win the election, she held numerous positions in New Jersey's state government before her death in 1983.

Women's increasing confidence in the workplace and political office also extended to the athletic field. "The Modern Girl Has Gone Mad for Athletics," trumpeted a headline in the August 1922 edition of the *Atlantic City Sunday Press*. "In less than 50 years, the girl who swooned at the sight of blood has been replaced by the girl who drives her own car, rides her own horse and has her own row," the article proclaimed. "The gentle woman no longer goes in for attacks of 'the vapors'; she no longer holds all forms of physical activity unmaidenly. The reverse is true with a vengeance."[93] The story went on to note that women were drawn to track and field, fencing, tug-of-war and "even the ancient and exciting sport of javelin throwing."

Female athletic competitions drew enthusiastic crowds, as noted in a June 1925 edition of the *Paterson News*. Some of the top women contenders in the East were preparing to meet at Sandy Hill Park to fight it out for places on a team of ten that would participate in national championships held in Pasadena, California.

"Champions, ex-champions and would-be contenders for high athletic honors will be among those who toe the mark on the various events Saturday

Congresswoman Mary Norton (*right*) was only one of the female luminaries active in New Jersey's political scene in the 1920s. She is seen here with activist Thelma Parkinson at the 1932 Democratic Convention.

afternoon and from present indications there are going to be some records smashed to smithereens for each and every entrant is in tip-top condition for the big event," the story noted. The event was described as "the biggest and best thing, athletically speaking, to be presented to the fans of the city in many moons." Events included the javelin throw, discus throw and thirty-yard dash.[94]

Even combative sports such as boxing held their appeal. "While most girls desire to be movie stars, society belles, stenographers or the like," according to a 1925 news report, fifteen-year-old Claire Pinlozik of Newark yearned to be a professional boxer. "She is already an amateur and has cleaned up everything in her neighborhood, boys and girls alike," the article reported. "Now she aims for the prize-ring and she claims she will be the first of her sex to make the grade."[95]

Women undoubtedly won numerous accolades for their achievements during the '20s, but there was a darker side to their time in the limelight. Weighing against the positive triumphs were some unsavory stories during the decade.

Left: Minnie Wohlbert, throwing a discus at a Paterson event.

Right: According to a 1925 news report, fifteen-year-old Newark girl Claire Pinlozik yearned to be a professional boxer.

The "radium girls" were women who entered the factory workforce during World War I to paint luminous dials on watches for the military at the United States Radium Corporation's factory in Orange, New Jersey. The work was delicate, and workers were advised by management to lick their brushes to create a fine point and so speed up production. On breaks, some painted their nails with the supposedly harmless luminous substance for entertainment.

As the years went by, the watch face painters developed illnesses, including anemia, brittle bones and "radium jaw," a grotesque deterioration of the jawbone, and gained the name "radium girls." In 1925, it was concluded that their condition was due to their work with radium, and they hired a lawyer, who filed a complaint against the company in 1927. The case moved slowly but got nationwide headlines and was arbitrated out of court. Five women received $10,000 cash, payment of all medical bills and a $600-a-month annuity for the rest of their lives. The last one died in the mid-1930s.

On the religious front, Alma White was one of the most prominent women in New Jersey and became infamous for her unbridled support of the white supremacist Ku Klux Klan. Born Mollie Alma Bridwell, she

Right: Katherine Shaub epitomized the story of the "radium girls."

Below: The abandoned radium paint building in the 1960s. Today, it is a vacant lot.

Opposite: Zarephath, New Jersey, Alma White's cult headquarters.

taught in a Methodist seminary and married seminarian Kent White—an occasion that facilitated her new identity. She dropped her last name and became Alma White.

The Whites established a church in Denver, but Alma apparently separated from Kent and became estranged from Methodism as well. In 1907, she moved to New Jersey, where she founded the Pillar of Fire Church on a donated farm in the Somerset community of Zarephath. White was ordained a bishop of her own church by a traveling Methodist evangelist. She then established her own Bible school, Zarephath Academy, on the farm. Zarephath dispatched evangelical recruiters across the country. Her religious community was labeled by a Red Bank, New Jersey newspaper as an "experiment in communism as well as religion" following revival services adherents held at Port Monmouth in 1921.

Bishop White, described by *Time* magazine as having "the mien of an inspired laundress," was a fierce feminist, but only in the service of white Protestant women. She was strongly anti-Catholic, anti-Semitic and anti-immigrant and a prominent Ku Klux Klan advocate. The Klan reciprocated with generous donations. White believed the Klan would help attain her goal of liberating white Protestant womanhood while keeping

ACADEMY, PUBLISHING AND ADMINISTRATION BUILDINGS.
Zarephath Academy (Pillar of Fire), Zarephath, N. J.

Left: Alma White.

Right: Alma White's *Good Citizen*, July 1926.

minorities and people of other religions "in their place." She praised the organization in her books and pamphlets, including her newsletter, *The Good Citizen*.

White's association with the Klan waned in the 1930s, when the organization became besieged by scandals involving high-level officials. She continued, however, to promote her ideology of intolerance for religious and racial minorities. At the time of her death in 1946, she had expanded her sect to an estimated four thousand followers.

Another member of New Jersey's female rogues' gallery was Mildred E. Gillars. In 1928, using the name "Mrs. Barbara Elliot," she walked into the office of the *Camden Courier Post*, known for its affinity for sensational stories, and announced emotionally that her "runaway husband Charles Elliot," last seen in Camden, had abandoned her and the infant in her womb.[96]

Gillars/Elliot stayed at the Hotel Walt Whitman, and the next morning, she called the desk clerk and asked him to go to her room. He did and found a complex suicide note, which made the front page of the *Courier Post*. The Camden police were advised, and on the morning of October 19, 1928, an officer patrolling the bridge to Philadelphia saw a female—Gillars—take off her coat and dangle a foot off the bridge. He grabbed her as she leaned toward the water, 130 feet below. Gillars was taken to police headquarters, where she was met by a mob of journalists and photographers. In police court, she maintained her right to commit suicide. That story made the front page, and she was kept in protective custody for a week.

Her "husband," a New York writer whose real name was John Ramsey, showed up at the *Courier Post* the following day, claiming that he was Charles Elliot, and was escorted to the police station, where his "wife" dramatically staged a fainting spell on his arrival. Presented with accumulated evidence throwing doubt on their story, Ramsey quickly confessed that he and Gillars had been offered seventy-five dollars each by a public relations firm to stage an event to publicize a movie titled *Unwanted Children*. Gillars then "confessed that her leaping and loving and sobbing and fainting were a hoax."

In police court, Gillars apologized for her hoax. She and her pretend husband were sentenced to three months in jail, but the sentence was suspended when they agreed to leave town immediately. Unfortunately, the motion picture publicity firm hadn't forwarded their salaries, and Gillars and Ramsey were broke. Local newspaper boys, whose sales had peaked because of the story, took pity, however, and "chipped in" to help the duo get home. One lad told them, "You did your best to put it over," adding that the show "was worth carfare back to New York," which was $12.75.

Gillars's escapades were an example of women's increasing involvement in crime during the '20s. "In every section of the United States women accelerating the crime wave are being forced to appear in courts to defend themselves against criminal charges," stated a 1922 news report in the *Press of Atlantic City*. "Women bootleggers are making difficult the enforcement of the Volstead Act. On the borders they are smuggling liquor into the United States and in the cities, women are arrested frequently for distilling and selling liquor."[97]

As part of the effort to combat the crisis, women were recruited into the ranks of law enforcement. "Female Detectives and Deputy United States Marshals to Be Pitted Against Increasing Army of Female

Mildred Gillars, principal character at the heart of the 1928 Camden scam.

Bandits, Bootleggers, Gamblers and Thieves" trumpeted a 1922 newspaper article. The story noted that nearly one hundred women were on the rolls of the Department of Justice as deputy United States marshals, functioning mostly as clerical workers.

Another negative aspect of the female experience during the 1920s was the struggle of minority women who faced the additional albatross of discrimination. Many, such as Hackensack teacher Nellie Morrow Parker, waged a valiant battle against the era's rampant prejudice. Hired by the Hackensack school district in 1922 as the first Black public school teacher in Bergen County, Parker faced a barrage of criticism and harassment from groups such as Daughters of the American Revolution and Ku Klux Klan. About 1,500 parents signed a petition protesting Parker's assignment to teach white students, and in response, the school reassigned her to Black pupils.

Tempers flared at a September 1923 school board meeting, where T.B. Jones, representing the African American community, castigated education officials. Jones claimed that "it was a gross insult to the [Black] residents of Hackensack, who have endeavored to boost the city along and were taxpayers, and still failed to obtain their rights, to have Miss Morrow segregated to teaching a class of her own race," according to coverage in the *Record*.[98]

Parker endured numerous indignities during the early years of her career, including a Klan parade that culminated with a burning cross in the lot next to her home. Despite her travails, Parker, who was described in news reports as "popular" and a "competent teacher," persevered and remained in the Hackensack school district for forty-two years, retiring at age sixty-nine.

Although the woman of the 1920s made great strides in many arenas, she is perhaps best remembered in popular culture as the fast-talking, chain-smoking flapper who shocked polite society with her boldness and audacity. A columnist in the *Bayonne Evening News* and *Bayonne Review* lamented the fact that many older women were adopting the frivolous attitudes and demeanor of teenage flappers.

"There isn't anything more tiresome, to speak lightly about it, than the flapper of forty," wrote columnist Winifred Black. "The woman who finds herself earnestly mimicking the voice, mannerisms and dress of the poor little flapper girls of any age should look out for herself. The adoption of the crass stupidity of the silly years is too much of a strain on anyone who has reached years of discretion."[99]

Women were sharply divided on some of the characteristics of the modern woman, particularly her penchant for cigarettes. The habit was rife

Women's liberation—sort of. Flappers publicly drinking alcohol, or pretending to.

among the younger female set, according to a March 1921 edition of the *Jersey Observer and Journal.*

"It is a well-known fact that many of the younger social set of the Bergen section and indeed all over the country smoke cigarettes, if Dame Rumor is to be believed," the news report observed. "It has been said that one of the young matrons in the Bergen section, who drives her auto, has been seen in the early evening dinner hour with a lighted cigarette in one hand and the other at the steering wheel of her car as she approached the Hudson Boulevard."[100]

Women surveyed by the newspaper had mixed reactions to the smoking trend. Mrs. C.P. Eaton, vice chairman of the Hudson County Republican Committee, was vehemently opposed to the fad. "I think it is one of those things they can do without and they needn't follow the men in that respect," she said.

Mrs. H. Otto Wittpenn agreed. "It isn't feminine, and I do not think that the best type of American women smoke," she said. "There is a certain cheapness about it and I should hate very much to think of a daughter of mine doing such a thing."

When you were a rich lady, you could have a maid light your cigarette, although the Depression was, unbeknownst to you, right around the corner.

Some of those interviewed thought women should be able to enjoy a cigarette—within reason. "I do not think young girls should smoke, but I do sanction the smoking of cigarettes by older women with their husbands and in their homes," said Mrs. Palmer Campbell of Hoboken. "I think it companionable, nerve quieting and restful for a woman to smoke at dinner or during the evening with her husband, but I do not approve of doing so in a public restaurant."

Alcohol was another favorite vice of the emancipated woman. Parents and preachers feared the consumption of liquor was an increasing problem among young people, including teenage girls. Speaking to a group of Atlantic City high school students in 1929, Reverend Albert G. Butzer referred to a statement by a Chicago school official, who observed that "half of the girls above sixteen accept this as their rule for a 'standard party': an auto ride, a dance at a road house, and a bottle of gin or 'moonshine.'"

Butzer voiced his concern that "all too many of our young people think it's smart to carry a hip flask around with them or else to imbibe from such a flask when it is offered to him."

Young girls were in particular danger when cavorting with their male peers, Butzer warned. "Given a half-dozen high school girls and fellows and a high-powered motor car and several bottles of bootleg liquor and you have one of the most dangerous combinations which it is possible to have," he said.[101]

Despite the brouhaha over morals, dress and drinking, New Jersey women made serious strides in the 1920s. They set the stage for future advances on the state and national level.

Women's accomplishments and the unfolding future possibilities were the focus of a 1924 meeting of the Woman's Republican Club in Glen Rock. The keynote speaker, Mrs. Raymond Brown, managing editor of a periodical run by women, noted that one of women's greatest accomplishments was winning the right to vote, giving them the chance to elevate the political process.

"There has been much abuse of political party loyalty by men in the past, and so far women have not adopted the masculine attitude that everything done by the party is perfect," Brown said. "They refuse to back a bad measure simply because a man of their own party endorses it."

The next crucial step, Brown observed, was to establish true parity with their male counterparts. "The next job for women is to persuade men to let them work with them as political partners…and to convince men that they can really help in the difficult work of governing in this country," she said.

Certainly, the road ahead was bumpy and fraught with setbacks. Women in New Jersey and across the country would labor to establish equal footing with men on all fronts. A strong foundation for this battle was set in the 1920s, when women expanded their horizons and began to pull away from the docile nineteenth-century stereotypes that held them at bay.

Behind the frivolous façade of flappers, fashion and social freedom, a groundswell of progress set the stage for the momentous achievements to come.

AFTERWORD

And so, as the decade came to a close, Edward I. Edwards, the New Jersey governor at the opening of the era who promised to find a way around Prohibition and keep the state legally as "wet as the Atlantic Ocean," lay dead in his bed in Jersey City.

In the years following the 1920s, New Jersey and the nation became unrecognizable to those who had lived through the cultural and social turmoil of the decade. The Great Depression of 1929 crashed the stock market, and many affluent people, including Edwards, lost their entire fortunes, while those still wealthy pushed successfully to end Prohibition and avoid higher income taxes. Herbert Hoover, president at the time, was a decent man, but the situation was beyond him.

The subsequent collapse of the entire economy affected most of the general population, and the climate "dust bowl" disaster of the Midwest created caravans of the impoverished heading off to California and blew dust east to Trenton.

And then came Franklin D. Roosevelt. "FDR," the former governor of New York, while far from perfect, would be the man of the hour, and a 100,000-person crowd at Sea Girt, New Jersey, organized by Hudson County Democratic Party political boss Frank Hague, held immediately after the Democratic Convention in Chicago, gave him a boost on his way.

With Roosevelt in office, his New Deal to extend government assistance to the economy and the unemployed began to take shape as the most significant transition in American history. The effect, like the cause of the debacle it was meant to address, was and continues to be debated by economists down to the present day, but highly visible public projects including, in New Jersey, bridges, tunnels and the socially experimental town of Jersey Homesteads, coupled with Roosevelt's personal charisma, carried him into unprecedented third and fourth presidential terms. The many people who got jobs were eternally grateful—and showed it on Election Day.

FDR's initial decade in office ended with another massive political and cultural transformation when German World War I veteran Adolf Hitler, who had taken over his country, started another war. We all know what happened then—and once more, New Jersey came to the center of the stage—but that is a story for another day.

NOTES

Introduction

1. For a look at the state in the years immediately preceding the 1920s, see Bilby, *New Jersey: A Military History*, 178–92.

Chapter 1

2. Mappen and Lurie, eds., *Encyclopedia of New Jersey*, Edward J. Connors, "Edward Irving Edwards," 243.
3. *Penn's Grove Record*, September 12, 1919.
4. *Asbury Park Press*, October 25, 1919.
5. *Paterson News*, October 19, 1919.
6. Mappen and Lurie, eds., *Encyclopedia of New Jersey*, Jonathan Lurie, "Woodrow Wilson," 377–78.
7. Ibid., Sheila Cowing and Amelia Fay, "Alice Paul," 620–21.
8. Green, "Madman in the White House."
9. Tyler, "100-Year Extinction Panic Is Back."
10. Mindel, "Getting the Job Done or Taking the Jobs?"; Krugman, "No, Immigrants Aren't Poisoning the Blood of Our Country."
11. Mappen and Lurie, eds., *Encyclopedia of New Jersey*, Henry Bischoff, "Immigration," 402–5; Shaw, *Immigration and Ethnicity in New Jersey History*, 10.

12. Federal Writers' Project, *New Jersey*, 73–74; Lender, *One State in Arms*, 76, 78.

13. New Jersey State Archives.

14. Mappen and Lurie, eds., *Encyclopedia of New Jersey*, Ethel M. Washington, "Gaetano Bresci," 97.

15. History, "Palmer Raids," www.fbi.gov/history/famous-cases/palmer-raids.

16. Hicks and Stuart, *John Reed*, 1.

17. *Trenton Times*, August 1, 11, 1921; *New Brunswick Home News*, August 20, 1921; *Bridgewater Courier-News*, September 21, 1921.

18. Shaw, *Immigration and Ethnicity in New Jersey History*, 49–50.

19. Bilby and Ziegler, *Rise and Fall of the Ku Klux Klan in New Jersey*, 104.

20. Mappen and Lurie, eds., *Encyclopedia of New Jersey*, Joseph Francis Mahoney, "Silzer, George Sebastian," 744–45.

21. Ibid.

22. *New York Times*, June 29, 1923; *New Brunswick Home News*, September 9, 1923.

23. *New York Times*, October 17, 1940.

24. Baker, "DNA Is Said to Solve a Mystery of Warren Harding's Love Life."

25. Shribman, "What America Can Still Learn from Calvin Coolidge."

26. Ibid.

27. Mappen and Lurie, eds., *Encyclopedia of New Jersey*, Carmela Karnoutsos, "Mary Teresa Norton," 589.

28. Bilby and Ziegler, *Unforgettable New Jersey Characters*, 23–24.

29. Bilby and Ziegler, *Rise and Fall of the Ku Klux Klan in New Jersey*, 108.

30. Mappen and Lurie, eds., *Encyclopedia of New Jersey*, Maxine Lurie, "Morgan Foster Larson," 456–57.

31. Ibid.

32. *New York Times*, January 27, 1932.

Chapter 2

33. Linderoth, *Prohibition on the North Jersey Shore*, 28.

34. Bilby, "Adventures in the Regular Army at the Turn of the Century," 4–10.

35. BI Report of F.A. Gaborino, August 20, 1917, Old German Files 1909–1921, #33658 NA, accessed through Fold3.com.

36. Ibid.

37. *New York Times*, January 15, 1924.

38. Linderoth, *Prohibition on the North Jersey Shore*, 22–24, 37–39.

39. Ibid., 46–50; Mappen and Saretzky, *Boot Legger Era*.

40. Bilby and Ziegler, *Rise and Fall of the Ku Klux Klan in New Jersey*, 57–60.

41. *Camden Courier Post*, May 18, 1925.
42. *Asbury Park Press*, December 26, 1923.
43. *Camden Courier Post*, May 18, 1925.
44. International Newsreel photo caption, May 7, 1925.
45. *Red Bank Register*, July 9, 1924.
46. *New York Times*, September 24, 1930; R.C. Miller, Chief of Police, Atlantic City, to Frederick M.P. Pearse, Secretary to the Governor, August 20, 1923, Governor George S. Silzer Papers, Box 31, Folder 178, New Jersey State Archives.
47. Mappen and Saretzky, *Boot Legger Era*; *Red Bank Register*, May 25, 1921.
48. Ibid.
49. *Red Bank Register*, October 1, 1930.
50. Mappen, *Jerseyana*.

Chapter 3

51. *Red Bank Register*, September 20, 1921.
52. *Press of Atlantic City*, September 21, 1921.
53. *Press of Atlantic City*, August 23, 1921; *Camden Courier Post*, August 13, 1921.
54. Oklahoma Historical Society, www.okhistory.org.
55. *Pittsfield Massachusetts and Berkshire County Eagle*, August 10, 1921.
56. *New York Times Herald*, August 4, 1921.
57. Thurlow, "Newark's Sculpture."
58. Hurst, "How New Jersey Became the Birthplace of the Movie Industry."

Chapter 4

59. *Central New Jersey Home News*, June 25, 1926.
60. *Asbury Park Evening Press*, January 16, 1924.
61. *Central Jersey Home News*, August 8, 1920.
62. *Bayonne Times*, November 30, 1927.
63. *Passaic Daily Herald*, November 14, 1927.
64. Ibid.
65. *Passaic Daily Herald*, February 27, 1924.
66. *Ridgewood Herald*, July 1, 1926.
67. Ibid.

68. *Monmouth Inquirer*, July 1, 1926.
69. Ibid.
70. *Morning Post*, March 14, 1929.
71. *Paterson Morning Call*, April 9, 1929.
72. *Bergen Evening Record*, November 28, 1926.
73. *Press of Atlantic City*, January 13, 1946.
74. Email conversation with James Cameron.
75. *Press of Atlantic City*, June 8, 1924.
76. Ibid.
77. *Jersey Observer and Journal*, April 10, 1922.
78. *Camden Morning Post*, August 14, 1923.
79. Ibid.
80. Ibid.
81. Ibid.
82. *Long Branch Daily Record*, November 15, 1926.

Chapter 5

83. *Central New Jersey Home News*, January 19, 1922.
84. Ibid.
85. *Press of Atlantic City*, March 12, 1929.
86. Ibid.
87. *Central New Jersey Home News*, September 9, 1922.
88. *Bayonne Times*, November 14, 1925.
89. *Press of Atlantic City*, March 12, 1929.
90. *Central New Jersey Home News*, March 22, 1923.
91. *Central New Jersey Home News*, October 29, 1925.
92. *Press of Atlantic City*, March 4, 1924.
93. *Atlantic City Sunday Press*, August 20, 1922.
94. *Paterson News*, June 18, 1925.
95. *Bergen Record*, October 2, 1827.
96. *Camden Courier Post*, October 29, 1928.
97. *Press of Atlantic City*, March 3, 1922.
98. *The Record*, September 11, 1923.
99. *Bayonne Evening News and Bayonne Review*, October 2, 1923.
100. *Jersey Observer and Journal*, March 23, 1921.
101. *Ridgewood Herald*, May 3, 1929.

BIBLIOGRAPHY

Books

Allen, Frederick Lewis. *Only Yesterday: An Informal History of the 1920s*. Chicago: University of Illinois Press, 1980.

Bilby, Joseph G. *New Jersey: A Military History*. Yardley, PA: Westholme Publishing, 2017.

Bilby, Joseph, and Harry Ziegler. *Asbury Park: A Brief History*. Charleston, SC: The History Press, 2009.

————. *The Rise and Fall of the Ku Klux Klan in New Jersey.* Charleston, SC: The History Press, 2019.

————. *Unforgettable New Jersey Characters: Heroes, Scoundrels, Politicians and More.* Charleston, SCK The History Press, 2022.

Cranmer, H. Jerome. *New Jersey in the Automobile Age: A History of Transportation.* New York: D. Van Nostrand, 1964.

Federal Writers' Project. *New Jersey: A Guide to Its Present and Past*. Washington, D.C., 1939.

Hicks, Granville, and John Stuart. *John Reed: The Making of a Revolutionary*. New York: Macmillan, 1936.

Kuntsler, William M. *The Hall Mills Murder Case: The Minister and the Choir Singer*. New York: William Morrow & Co., 1964.

Lender, Mark. *One State in Arms: A Short Military History of New Jersey*. Trenton: New Jersey Historical Commission, 1991.

Linderoth, Matthew R. *Prohibition on the North Jersey Shore: Gangsters on Vacation.* Charleston, SC: The History Press, 2010.

Mappen, Marc. *Jerseyana: The Underside of New Jersey History.* New Brunswick, NJ: Rutgers University Press, 1992.

Mappen, Marc, and Maxine Lurie, eds. *Encyclopedia of New Jersey.* New Brunswick, NJ: Rutgers University Press, 2004.

New Jersey History Committee. *Outline History of New Jersey.* New Brunswick, NJ: Rutgers University Press, 1950.

Shaw, Douglas V. *Immigration and Ethnicity in New Jersey History.* Trenton: New Jersey Historical Commission, 1994.

Willever, Daniel. *Made in Paterson: The Life and Legacy of U.S. Senator William Hughes.* Self-published, 2023.

Zimmer, Kenyon. *Immigrants Against the State: Yiddish and Italian Anarchism in America.* Champaign: University of Illinois Press, 2015.

Articles

Baker, Peter. "DNA Is Said to Solve a Mystery of Warren Harding's Love Life." *New York Times,* August 12, 2015.

Bilby, Joseph G. "Adventures in the Regular Army at the Turn of the Century." *Military Images Magazine* 1, no. 5 (March–April 1980): 4–10.

Green, Dominic. "The Madman in the White House: Sigmund Freud, Ambassador Bullitt, and the Lost Psychobiography of Woodrow Wilson." *Wall Street Journal,* December 8, 2023.

Hurst, Carol. "How New Jersey Became the Birthplace of the Movie Industry." *Variety,* December 9, 2022.

Krugman, Paul. "No, Immigrants Aren't Poisoning the Blood of Our Country." *New York Times,* November 14, 2023.

Mindel, Maia. "Getting the Job Done or Taking the Jobs? Immigrants Good or Bad." Substack.com, May 18, 2023.

Shribman, David M. "What America Can Still Learn from Calvin Coolidge." *Wall Street Journal,* July 27, 2023.

Thurlow, Fearn. "Newark's Sculpture: A Survey of Public Monuments and Memorial Statuary." *Newark Museum Quarterly* (Winter 1975).

Tyler, Austin Harper. "The 100-Year Extinction Panic Is Back, Right on Schedule." *New York Times,* January 31, 2024.

Other Sources

Mappen, Marc, and Gary D. Saretzky, curators. *The Boot Legger Era: Prohibition in New Jersey*. Monmouth County Library, 2013.

Newspapers

Asbury Park Evening Press
Asbury Park Press
Bayonne Evening Times and Bayonne Review
Bayonne Times
Bergen Evening Record
Camden Morning Post
Central New Jersey Home News
Courier News
Jersey Observer and Jersey Journal
Long Branch Daily Record
Monmouth Inquirer
Morning Post
Passaic Daily Herald
Paterson Morning Call
Paterson News
Penn's Grove Record
Press of Atlantic City
Ridgewood Herald

ABOUT THE AUTHORS

JOSEPH G. BILBY received his BA and MA degrees in history from Seton Hall University. He served as a lieutenant in the First Infantry Division's First MP Company in Vietnam, retired as an investigations supervisor from the New Jersey Department of Labor and is now part-time assistant curator of the National Guard Militia Museum of New Jersey in Sea Girt. He is the author, coauthor or editor of twenty-two books, two of which are on the New Jersey State Historical Commission's list of "101 Great New Jersey Books," and a freelance writer and historical consultant. He served on the New Jersey Civil War Sesquicentennial Committee and was editor of several of its publications, including the award-winning *New Jersey Goes to War*, a book on 150 of the state's Civil War–era personalities. He coauthored *The Rise and Fall of the Ku Klux Klan in New Jersey*, *A History of Submarine Warfare Along the Jersey Shore* and other works. Bilby has been awarded the Jane Clayton Award for contributions to Monmouth County (NJ) history; an Award of Merit from the New Jersey Historical Commission for his *New Jersey: A Military History*, which covers the military story of the Garden State from 1607 to the present; and the prestigious Richard J. Hughes Prize from the state historical commission for his work.

HARRY ZIEGLER graduated from Monmouth University with a BA degree in English. He went to work as a reporter for the *Asbury Park Press*, at the time one of the largest newspapers in the state. He rose to the position of managing editor but at that point realized that the days of large newspaper influence were waning. He resigned his position to take a teaching job, acquired an MA in education and is currently the principal of Saint Thomas Acquinas high school, a private academy. He has worked with Bilby, his brother-in-law, on a number of books, including *A History of Submarine Warfare Along the Jersey Shore* and *The Rise and Fall of the Ku Klux Klan in New Jersey*.